FINDING ANCHORS

How to Bring Stability to Your Life
Following a Cancer Diagnosis

FINDING ANCHORS

How to Bring Stability to Your Life Following a Cancer Diagnosis

Rick Bergh, M.Div., CT

Author of *Taking Notice* and *Looking Ahead*

Finding Anchors

Copyright © 2015 by Rick Bergh

Published by
Beacon Mount Publishing
#18 West Chapman Place
Cochrane, Alberta, T4C 1J9, Canada
www.rickbergh.com   www.beaconmountpublishing.com

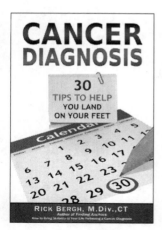

Go to www.rickbergh.com/cancertips for your free copy

ISBN 978-0-9947962-2-6 (paperback)
ISBN 978-0-9947962-9-5 (ePub)
ISBN 978-1-988082-05-9 (Mobi)
ISBN 978-1-988082-00-4 (audio)
ISBN 978-1-988082-08-0 (hardcover)

Author's Note
The names, details and circumstances may have been changed to protect the privacy of those mentioned in this publication.

This publication is not intended as a substitute for the advice of health care professionals.

Printed and bound in the United States of America.

Dedication

This book is dedicated to Ken and Ruth Koskinen, my other mom and dad, who blessed me with their daughter, Pam.

And to Pam, who continued to live life beyond what I thought possible.

Acknowledgements

This book represents the realization of a life-long dream to share with others what I have learned over the past 30 years from hundreds of people. I have been privileged to walk alongside them as a pastor, counselor, and friend. I would like to thank each of them for being the real educators in my life as I journeyed with them. It is where the rubber meets the road that you learn the most and they have taught me far more than my formal education ever did. If the principles in this book are practical, useful or helpful, it is because they are rooted in the many experiences of these dear ones.

It was in Westlock, Alberta, that Pam was first diagnosed with cancer. This small town of 5000 people reached out with compassion and care. A special thank you to Peace Lutheran Community Church and Flatbush Community Church — you were instrumental in helping us survive.

Thank you to my four children: Devon, Keeara, Larissa and Landon. You kept encouraging me to write and believed that I had a significant story to share that would be helpful to others. I have great kids! I love them so much.

I want to thank all of my extended family for their support, encouragement and love. I cannot believe how blessed I am to have such an amazing family.

I want to thank Steve and Bill Harrison and their team at Quantum Leap Publishing and Marketing. Their mentoring and coaching were key in publishing my first book (and many more to come).

I want to thank my editor, Rhonda Fleming of RJF Writing Services, for her wisdom, guidance and patience. You were a gift sent my way. I appreciate your support and belief in my work.

I want to thank my wife Erica, whom I married on July 31, 2010, in Montreal, Quebec. To have been blessed twice with wonderful wives is still beyond my comprehension. Erica has added so much to this book with her creative use of words and amazing feedback. She was my first line editor. I could not have done this without her. I love you, Erica.

I want to thank you, God. More than anything, I want to please You with these words, because ultimately it's Your story in me thus far. I only want to share what might be helpful to others as they journey through life, a world with its challenges and its beautiful moments. I'm just one person whom You love, because I know how much You love each individual. You are ultimately my audience of One. So do as you please with these words.

Contents

Preface

A cancer diagnosis can quickly sweep us out to sea. There we can drift unknowingly into uncharted waters and be subjected to changing weather, sudden storms and unexpected obstacles.

Knowing our anchors and putting them down is an important decision, and one we need to proactively consider as we transition into new territory.

This book shares 17 anchors that can help stabilize you and your family as you move into turbulent waters. You decide which ones you can best integrate into your life. Some of these may already be familiar to you. Others may be new—but they are all anchors you may want to consider.

These are anchors I discovered and personally implemented in my life as a result of my wife Pam's cancer diagnosis at 42 years of age. The principles behind each "anchor" helped our family of six (Pam, myself and our four children) as we entered into rough seas. In part, you will discover our family's story in these pages, but I encourage you to glean what you can from our experiences, good and bad, and make it your own.

In addition to my experience with Pam, I have also learned about these anchors over the past 30 years from the hundreds of people I have had the opportunity to work with professionally following a cancer diagnosis—both as a pastor and as a counselor.

I feel honored and humbled to be able to be in your boat as an educator at this strategic time. Providing solid, practical information people can intentionally put into practice is the mandate of my work and this book. I hope you find some anchors that work for you, your family and your community.

If these anchors have helped you or if you have discovered others that have helped you, please let us know and become part of our community at www.rickbergh.com/findinganchors.

Introduction

It was a just a normal day in the life of the Bergh Family. There was the typical rush to get the kids off to school—sharing one bathroom between four children. Lunches were made. Binders were in backpacks. Quick reminders to the kids about their daily activities. We were an active, busy and happy family.

My wife, Pam, was usually involved in the morning routine, but not today. The night before, I had taken her to the hospital for minor surgery—day surgery, really. The previous day, the doctor had told her that there was a small cyst on one of her ovaries. Since the hospital was an hour south of where we lived, I took her there the night before the scheduled surgery. She would have surgery in the morning and I'd pick her up later that afternoon.

"Say hi to Mom," Keeara, our eldest daughter, chirped as she left. "Yeah, tell Mom that we love her and are praying for her," Larissa added. The others agreed. "Okay, kids, love you! Have a good day and we'll see you at dinner," I said. After giving them each a hug and watching them disappear out the door, I put my coat on and walked toward our large, red minivan in the driveway.

"I missed Pam this morning," I thought to myself. "I'm exhausted just getting all the kids organized! She's so good at it." I couldn't wait to pick up Pam and get her back home to our family, where she thrived.

Pam was an awesome mom. I knew that she would be the minute I first met her back in college. We were both in the choir. I spotted the back of her head as I sat perched on the back riser, singing in the bass section, looking down toward the front row. I couldn't help but notice a head of gorgeous, thick, blond hair near the front. The angle at which I sat didn't afford me a glimpse of her face though. That came at the end of choir practice when she turned to speak to a girl behind her. "Wow!" I thought. "She is beautiful! And she won't last long around here." So I devised my game plan.

Since I was living off-campus as a mature student (debatable), I wouldn't have the opportunity to meet her in the cafeteria or around campus. So I knew I would have to be strategic in my plan.

I waited patiently until the next choir practice when I'd make my move. As soon as rehearsal was over, I elbowed my way past the other basses to the edge of the riser. "Hey! What's your hurry?" someone asked. "You'll see," I said in my usual cocky, self-confident manner.

As I made my way down, Pam was already at the front door, heading to the cafeteria for dinner. I hurried over to her, catching her before she left. "Hi! I'm Rick," I said. She turned to me and smiled, "My name's Pam," she replied. "Is this your first year?" I continued. "Yes," she answered, "I'm in Education." "This is my third year. I'm living off campus," I continued, not sure if I impressed her that much with this piece of information (considering I was still living with my mom and dad). "Can I walk with you?" I asked. So we spoke for a few minutes. She was shy, beautiful and kind. And I was smitten.

It wasn't long before we started dating and the vision of this wonderful woman becoming my wife and the mother of my children was already beginning to formulate in my mind. I had plans for this amazing woman!

Four years later we were married. Pam had finished her teaching degree and I was an intern pastor-in-training in Yellowknife, North West Territories. It was there that we began our married life together.

Now, six moves later, we were living in Westlock, a small farming community of 5000 people, in northern Alberta, Canada. It was June 4, 2003, one day after my 44th birthday. Pam and I had been married for nearly 20 years and had four children: Devon (17), Keeara (16), Larissa (14) and Landon (12). That morning I was driving down the highway to the hospital in St. Albert to pick up my wife and bring her home from her minor day surgery—just a small blip in our wonderful life. That's what I was thinking as I drove.

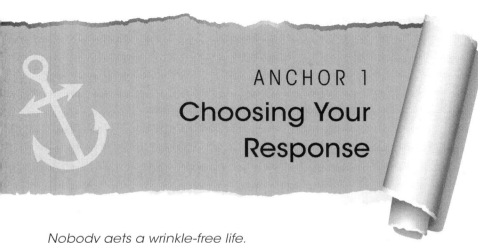

ANCHOR 1

Choosing Your Response

Nobody gets a wrinkle-free life.
– PAUL HENDERSON

A rriving in St. Albert an hour later, I turned into the hospital parking lot. I had been there numerous times before, usually visiting congregational members as a parish pastor. Hospitals were familiar to me. I knew the layout backwards and forwards and even had a clergy parking pass.

I knew what room Pam was in, so I quickly made my way toward the elevator and down the hall to where she was. I wanted to see how the surgery had gone and give her a kiss. More than anything, I just wanted to bring her home and return to my work and my normal life.

I bounced into the room with enthusiasm. Of the two beds in the room, Pam's was closest to the window. The curtain was closed around her, so I assumed she was resting following her early morning surgery.

As I poked my head around the edge of the curtain, she was sitting up in her bed. "Hi Honey!" I beamed. Then I stopped. "Haven't you had your surgery yet?" I asked. She began to speak, "They started to operate but..." then she was silent for a moment. "But then…" she tried to continue. "Rick, I have some news to share with you. Sit down," she said. My heart began to race. I was not even remotely close to being prepared for what I was about to hear. She took my hands and looked into my eyes as she had done so many times before. "They found some cancer," she said. "What?" I said, stunned. "Cancer? In *you*? No, that can't be right," I protested. "That wasn't just a cyst. I have ovarian cancer," she said. Up to that point, I had never even known anyone who had had ovarian cancer. "So… they can just remove it?" I asked hopefully. "Well, it's a little more complicated than that," Pam said, unwaveringly. "I have been scheduled for a hysterectomy in the next few days and then chemotherapy following a recovery period."

My eyes began to water. *Not Pam!* I thought to myself. Pam was the most clean-living person ever. She never drank or smoked. She cooked only healthy food. She was an emotionally-positive person who loved life and people. She was unselfish and giving. She was loved by everybody and extremely humble. *Not Pam! This can't be happening to me, to Pam, to our family!* the voice inside me screamed.

As I began to cry openly, I hugged Pam and said, "Pam, why you?" There was silence for a moment so I asked again, "Pam, why you?" I insisted. She looked up at me with those deep blue eyes that had captured my heart 24 years earlier and simply said, "Why *not* me, Rick?" I was incredulous. Had I heard correctly? "It could have been one of our daughters, one of our nieces, one of my sisters. But it's me. It's okay. We will get through this together and with God's help," Pam assured.

And then we prayed.

About half an hour later she said, "I'm a little tired. I'm going to rest. We have to wait for the doctor to discharge me, so why don't you go get yourself a coffee. I'll be fine." As I left her room, I looked at her and a myriad of thoughts flooded my mind: *How will I tell the kids? How will I tell her Mom and Dad?*

I have to confess that my first response to a cancer diagnosis was not as gracious as Pam's. I was immediately directing my questions and my anger toward God. "Why Pam, God? This can't be! This is not fair! This is not convenient. This is not right! Why did you let this happen?"

A diagnosis does not mean death, but my mind was already moving too far ahead: *What if Pam dies? This is my wife. How about the children? What about our life together? How about me? Pam is only 42 years old. There's so much ahead for us. We have plans. I didn't envision this. This can't be happening!*

As I made my way to the elevator, more confusing thoughts filled my head. Disbelief. Shock. Fear. It felt like someone had grabbed my heart and was squeezing it in a vise. I could barely hold back my tears as I rode the elevator down to the lobby.

I walked briskly at first and then I bolted for my car. Once inside, I grabbed the steering wheel with both hands and wept. I was terrified and had no idea what the future would hold — and Pam faced that same fear with, "Why *not* me?" Her courage astounded me.

For those of you reading this book, you may well recall your first reactions to the bad news. It is never fair that it's happening to you. Never fair. Cancer strikes people at every age — whether a child, parent, spouse, relative, friend, neighbor or co-worker. It always seems to come so unexpectedly.

Most cancer diagnoses seem to evoke one of two responses: "Why me?" or "Why not me?" Both are fair questions. Both reveal elements of shock, denial or disbelief. If you recently had a family member diagnosed with cancer, soon you will likely discover a variety of reactions from those who are told the bad news.

Sorting through the initial shock and intentionally deciding how you might approach the next step will be really important for you. It may take some time, but sooner or later you will need to ask the question: "So what's next? And what can I do about it?" Cancer doesn't wait for people to catch up. You will need to take some action and begin to put down some anchors to support you and your family along the way.

The truth is, we want to believe that cancer can't and won't happen to us—but sometimes it does. It happened to me and to our family. Pam's courageous journey began that day in the hospital room when she said "Why not me?" I'm sure it wasn't an easy phrase to say, nor was it an easy phrase to hear. But Pam made a choice that day—a choice to engage life and face this new challenge in a way that was both realistic and hopeful.

Cancer plays no favorites. It chooses people randomly. Now it had visited our family and I needed to learn what to "do" with it. How would I process this news? I realized that before I did anything, I'd need to reach out to those who were most important to me and begin to put into place the support that would allow us to live life fully following this diagnosis. Our life was not finished. But we did need to make some big adjustments as we transitioned. We needed to consider some anchors, and so will you if you are at a similar juncture in your life.

After coming to terms with Pam's sad news, I needed to drop another anchor to secure my way. "Who should I call?" I dialed my mom and dad.

Understanding Your Past

*Those who cannot remember the past
are condemned to repeat it.*
- GEORGE SANTAYANA

As I sat in my vehicle, knowing that Pam was resting in her hospital bed, it became clear to me that I needed to talk with someone about what had just happened. For the moment, this was about me managing what I was going through in response to a wife who had just been diagnosed with cancer. It was my reaction to this unexpected turn of events that had left me reeling.

I knew how much my mom and dad loved Pam and me, and I needed to call them. I was fortunate to have them in my life. I had learned so much from them growing up as one of their three children.

You learn so much from your parents. Not all children have happy family homes or parents who teach them important life skills that equip them for life's challenges and problems. Have you ever noticed how some people are able to transition through life's problems more smoothly than others? You wonder why they are able to get back on their feet so quickly following huge roadblocks and adapt so quickly.

Maybe you had parents who taught you by example how to transition well. You watched them; you listened to their wisdom, without even realizing at the time how those words would come into play in your own life later on; and now you copy them, usually without even being aware you are doing so.

Yes, I was blessed to have parents who taught me how to work through loss. So I knew they would be my first phone call.

Mom and Dad had taken care of my grandpa as he battled cancer. I was a student that summer and had come back to live at home. I saw how beautifully my mom and dad had interacted with and cared for Gramps, who was sick with terminal cancer. It was a privilege to be with Gramps in his last days, spending time with him and seeing how he dealt with his own cancer. It was a time of deep conversation, warm words, reminiscing, realistic expectations and intense hope for all of us. It's one thing to know people who have had cancer, it's quite another to live with someone who has cancer. I learned so much about caring for the terminally ill from that experience. I also knew that my parents would understand me at this particular juncture. I was looking for advice, support and encouragement as I maneuvered this unexpected turn in the road.

I needed someone to talk to about what I was going through, so I called my parents. I never realized how hard it would be to tell them this bad news. It seemed different when Dad told me he was going in for some cancer treatments. I suppose in some ways you expect some hiccups with your health when you get older, but Pam was only 42. My hand shook as I removed my cell phone from my pocket. I had comforted hundreds of people in my life as a minister and had been on the listening end of many difficult conversations. I had commiserated with people in their homes and had been invited to go with them to their doctor's office when the bad news about cancer was first shared. But to tell someone about my own loved one, about *this* cancer diagnosis, was very difficult. In fact, it was gut-wrenching.

I had not even told Mom or Dad about this day surgery because it wasn't going to be a big deal. I didn't want to bother them. They were going through enough on their own. I called their number on my cell phone. "Hi Mom. It's Rick," I began. "Hi Rick! How are you? Happy belated birthday!" she exclaimed. "Thanks, Mom," I replied and then continued without hesitation—all the careful rehearsal of my message dissolved as I blurted out: "Pam has cancer!" Silence followed. "Where are you, Rick?" Mom asked. "I'm in St. Albert at the hospital," I replied trying to hold back tears. "Dad and I will come right now." That's all that I needed to hear: "We will come right now." There was nothing they could say that would quiet my anxiety at that moment. But just having them present would be so good for me.

They arrived at the hospital about an hour later. As they came through the door, I walked over to them, hurled myself into their arms and cried. I was so glad to have them in my life.

Numerous times since that day, I have realized the importance of family origin when going through loss. Whether or not you are close to your family is not the issue. Some people are not close to their parents for a variety of reasons, but what they taught you about loss and transitioning through it is monumental when you experience loss in your own life. In this case, my parents modeled what it meant to "be there" rather than speak platitudes.

Whether we realize it or not, we are constantly acquiring information from our parents—some helpful, some not so helpful. No family unit is perfect. Examining why we respond the way we do and how our family of origin has impacted those responses is key. This requires a certain amount of vulnerability and self-awareness. We have to admit to ourselves the good things that our parents passed on as well as the bad. How did they respond to family deaths? Traumatic experiences? Were they able to reframe it? Or did loss become debilitating? How did it affect you and your siblings? Were they able to comfort you? Each other? Did they talk about it? Become sullen and silent? All these things from the past will come to bear on your response to loss now, as an adult.

If you didn't acquire healthy coping tools as a young person, you need to take responsibility now to do so and to build strategies that will be helpful to you in transition. This starts by taking an inner inventory and being honest with what happened in your family when you were a kid. That may sound like a lot of work, but it will pay off as you explore it now.

Exercise: Examining Your Past

Think back to the times when you went through difficult transitions while you were growing up. Chart these out on a piece of paper as a timeline. Take a few minutes to examine each one. Examples could include: divorce, financial struggles, death in the family, job loss, a move to a new location, loss of a friendship, difficult parting of a family member, a new career, pet loss or even the loss of a physical part of your body or declining health. Ask the following questions about each loss:

- What do I remember about this specific loss?
- Do I remember who was present?
- How did my parent(s) initially respond to the loss?
- How were feelings expressed in response to the loss?
- Was it just passed over quickly, becoming the "elephant in the room" that no one ever talked about again?
- Can you picture people speaking about the situation and communicating with each other?
- Did it seem healthy or not in retrospect?
- Did you see any harmful responses? Was there any abuse involved (addiction, substance abuse — alcohol, domestic violence or drug use)?

- Did you see any other coping mechanism utilized during this loss (religion, prayer, counseling, friendship)?
- Did it have an impact on your family finances?
- Can you recall how extended family members responded to the specific loss?
- How did you respond?
- How were decisions made? Who was involved in these decisions?
- On a scale from 1 (healthy) to 10 (toxic), how would you rate the transition of each loss that you described above?

As you reflect on these losses, you will see patterns beginning to form. Have you picked up any bad habits from your family of origin? What positive foundation can you point to from your family? In light of the information you have gleaned from your past experiences, what do you feel you need to add to your toolbox to help you in your loss? What do you need to get rid of?

Don't worry if you feel you are lacking some resources you need to manage this transition. Later in this book I will provide some tools that will really help you. What is important is that you recognize what you have in your toolbox to date and be open to acquiring some new coping skills.

If you took time to answer the above questions, then you have been courageous. You have made yourself vulnerable enough to discover something about yourself so many other people would not take time to consider for fear of what they might find. Just by doing the work, you have set down another important anchor from which you will operate.

Knowing Your Communication Style

Effective communication is 20% what you know and 80% how you feel about what you know.

– JIM ROHN

I brought Pam home later that afternoon. The children were all arriving home from after-school activities. Before supper, I called a family meeting. When we called a family meeting, it was usually to review our responsibilities in the home or to get input from the kids on bigger decisions that would involve the entire family. So the children were expecting a conversation about more mundane topics than the bomb that was about to hit them. They were not ready for this talk. Who would be — ever?

As Pam's husband, I was devastated by the bad news, but that was due, in large part, to the inner emotional contortions I felt as I anticipated the responses of our four children. I don't know how many tears rolled down my cheeks as I practiced how I would tell them about their mom's cancer diagnosis. I thought about each one of the children and how they might respond to the news. I reflected upon their unique personalities. I began to picture how each one would interact with their mom as a result of hearing the news. It's crazy what you think about when you're under emotional duress, but in my case, my mind went back to the time each one of them was born. I would picture Pam holding her precious newborn. She loved each one of them so much.

Jesus of Nazareth once shared a story about the importance of foundations. He talked about the importance of building your life on something that was firm and could weather the storms. He said, "Are you building your life on sand or on rock?" You quickly discover which it is when you receive an unwanted diagnosis. Pam and I knew what the foundational rocks were in our life. We had values that guided our life. As such, we decided it would be necessary to remind our children of those foundational principles as we lived life in one of those storms Jesus talked about.

I knew what those principles were, but as I told our four children, I would have to start with the storm first. I was not looking forward to telling the children and then seeing the look on their faces. It would be one of the most difficult and yet most intentional conversations I would ever have with my family.

Pam asked me to start the conversation and to be the one to tell the children about her cancer. She was always supportive. Even when I quit the ministry with no job and four young kids, she said, "I believe in you, Rick. Don't worry. If you think God wants you to step out into something new, I will totally support you. We will make it. I know you." She was my biggest cheerleader. As we gathered in the living room late that afternoon, Pam looked at me from across the room and I could feel her cheering me on. I needed those vibes from her like never before. I had to deliver to the children the most difficult news they had ever received to that point in their lives.

The kids knew me well. They knew my character. They knew their mom well—she was a very strong woman in so many ways. They had experienced the work of God in our life as a family and had seen the value of faith. We had many conversations prior to this one about living life to the fullest and a home built on honesty, truth and deep affection. Pam used to pray her children out the door every morning, placing the sign of the cross on their forehead to remind them of a God who had marked them forever and loved them deeply. I was wondering how they would respond to God now that their mom was diagnosed with cancer.

I felt weak as I began to share the news we had learned earlier that day. "Your mom has to have a different kind of surgery," I began. "The doctors have discovered cancer in her." I will never forget that moment. Time stopped. Eyes brimmed. Tears rolled. Lips quivered.

"Mom, are you going to be okay?" a frail voice asked. "I will be fine. God is with us," she assured. Pam always referred to her faith — it was natural and unrehearsed — it was her default and brought us hope.

"I need to have surgery to remove all of my 'woman stuff'," she said. "And then I'm going to go through some chemo treatments."

The word *chemo* was not an attractive word for us. Just six months earlier, one of Pam's best friends had died from breast cancer. The memory of that was still pretty fresh. All of my children were friends with her kids. They had seen the ugly side of cancer and the results this disease can bring.

"We need to be honest about this cancer," I continued. "Eventually Mom will lose her hair and people will talk. News will get out in this small community and people will wonder. We need to talk about it with people who are closest to us so they know. We also need to continue to live each day to the fullest," I said, trying to encourage myself as well.

"And we need to trust God," Pam piped up. "Let's always keep things in perspective."

All the children cuddled Pam that evening, each in their own way. We prayed together and then we went to sleep. I lay next to Pam and wondered about my future, not wanting to think about Pam dying, or what it would be like not to have her in my life. "Please God," I said, "please help us." For hours I wept silently on the inside and woke up exhausted to face a day of transition and the reality that I was married to a wife and mom who had cancer.

There are many people who are touched by a cancer diagnosis. Each one is certain to process the information in a specific manner based on their age, their relationship with the person and their specific communication style. In this chapter I will focus on how we communicate and how others might respond to a diagnosis and why it's important to consider these factors.

Have you ever noticed how some people will shut down following a difficult conversation while others will immediately respond by sharing their feelings, asking questions and offering opinions?

We all respond to news differently. Instead of getting upset by people's response to our diagnosis, we must appreciate and recognize that each person is different and each person's way needs to be accepted and honored.

Devon, our eldest son, holds his feelings very close to himself and needs time to process what is going on in his heart. His response to his mom's diagnosis was quiet and thoughtful. He said very little but we knew he was thinking deeply and processing things in his own way. We needed to give him space and check in with him from time to time. To force him to share what was going on would not have been helpful for him or for us.

Keeara quickly places difficult conversations in context. She always feels deeply for the person who is most impacted and seeks to reach out in some practical manner with words or actions that connect deeply with people. It was no different with her mom as she immediately took on some of the organizational tasks in our home and cared for the family. She would write encouraging notes to Pam and affirm her. This is how we recognized that Keeara was entering into the situation in a healthy way.

Larissa's tears flowed freely as soon as we told the family. She feels deeply for others. But she is also our family "researcher" and we knew that she would be on the Internet looking up information on Pam's illness right away. She responds by thinking things over and then comes to an intellectual understanding of the options. Based on the information she gleans, she comes to her own conclusions.

Landon's response to his mom's cancer diagnosis was to express his emotions openly and often. He's a huge extrovert, so he continued his natural communication patterns with his ongoing humorous remarks, positive words and warm physical touch. You would often find Landon cuddling his mom. We knew he was responding in a 'Landon-like' way by speaking clearly and honestly with his mom.

We had a good sense about how the kids might respond and they were true to themselves, but how could we begin to even think about all the different relationships — all those who needed to be told about the diagnosis — and discern the best way to tell each one? I know I really got tired of telling people about Pam's diagnosis, mostly because of people's reactions. Much of my energy went into emotionally supporting *other* people who found the news so difficult to process.

Perhaps you are struggling with how best to let people know you are struggling with cancer or have been recently diagnosed. The chapters on personality differences and love languages later in this book will help to provide some good information. But as a start, why not do a little bit of homework prior to telling people closest to you? Here are some ideas you may find helpful:

At the very least, these five areas are important for you to talk about with all those who are closest to you. How, when and where you decide to do this is in your court. Consider each person as you talk about these areas. Consider their personalities, the way they might respond to the news based on past experiences and how you might best tell them about the diagnosis.

a) You need to decide how you will let each person know about your cancer. How you decide to explain this is important. What words will you use? What metaphors might be helpful?

b) You need to be clear about the steps you are planning to take in order to deal with the cancer. Share a clear and direct plan about what you are going to do in the days to follow.

c) Remind them that their relationship with you is not going to change as a result of this cancer, but because you will be going through some treatments, it may need to be redefined depending on what you need to do and how you are feeling physically.

d) Foster hope within your family members and friends, reminding them of the values that are important to you and hold on to them as you work together in the future.

e) It is also important to let them know how often you will talk with them and keep them updated on the situation. This keeps the lines of communication open.

You'll have to prepare yourself for some immediate questions from some individuals—they will come and will come from many perspectives—as many questions as there are people. Know, too, that many emotions will flow from those whom you've told and that's okay. It's better to have open discussion with those who need to talk immediately than a family that doesn't communicate in the midst of the crisis. For others you may have to approach them later with the questions they really deep down want to ask but don't because of their communication style.

If someone's communication style is more direct, you may get the type of FAQ that is found in Column A. But if the person is more introverted, you may need to be the one to ask the questions and draw them out by using the questions in Column B. We experienced both types of questions within our own family:

Column A	Column B
Are you going to die?	Are you worried at all about me dying?
Is this partially my fault?	I hope you know this cancer has nothing to do with you.
Should I be home more often, instead of being with my friends?	It's okay for you to be with your friends.
Why did this happen?	Do you ever wonder why this happened to me?
Where is God in all this?	Do you ever wonder where God is in this stuff?
I'm angry and sad that this has happened.	Do you ever feel angry or sad about this cancer?

Be courageous and talk with your immediate family about your cancer diagnosis. Be sensitive to their responses and examine the specific relationship you have with that person. Expect different reactions and responses and be okay with each one as they process something that is also impacting their life as well as yours. Begin to recognize and use the most effective way for you to communicate with each one.

Involving Your Extended Family

To maintain a joyful family requires much from both the parents and the children. Each member of the family has to become, in a special way, the servant of the others.

– POPE JOHN PAUL II

P am's mom and dad are amazing people. We had almost lost her dad to a heart attack five years earlier and I think all of us were caught off guard by that unexpected event. It was a wake-up call. Pam's diagnosis was more than a wake-up call. It erupted into our lives so unexpectedly. There were no signs; she was outside of the age range that is associated with ovarian cancer; there was no history of cancer in her family; she lived a super-clean life; she had a positive outlook on life; and she was not a worrier. Thinking back, all I noticed was that Pam was a little more tired than her usual buoyant self. We thought nothing of it, considering her busy life and raising four kids.

I learned early in my ministry that many people choose to exclude extended family in their own cancer journey because of fear of interference, strong opinions or spousal disagreement. They may let them know what's happening initially but then choose to keep a "healthy" distance. "I don't want your mom here because she is so opinionated." "I don't want your dad here because he's always telling me what to do." "I don't want your sister here because she is over-the-top religious." Sound familiar?

A diagnosis is not the end, but it's a huge transition for a person and their family. The role of extended family is crucial in healthy living following a cancer diagnosis. It can be a vital anchor.

Pam's mom and dad were on vacation in Hawaii when all of this happened, so we decided to wait until they were back before we told them. I had tried to live my life as best as I could in the interim. Pam had gone in for surgery and was now in a period of healing and recovery prior to beginning her chemo treatments.

She had already told her two sisters about the cancer. In so many ways, Pam was the comforter to each one of *us* as she faced this with courage, communicating the diagnosis straight up, but following it with words of peace, trust and hope. She inspired us all with her positive attitude.

Where had she learned this optimism? From her mom and dad, who were amazingly faithful and prayerful people. With them, the cup was always half-full. I loved them so much. I had never met people as kind and generous to others. They were so solid and trusted in God's providence. But now I would be a messenger with the solemn task of delivering very difficult news about one of their own dear daughters.

I was the one picking up Pam's mom and dad at the airport. How would I tell her parents that the daughter THEY gave me and entrusted to MY care had cancer? And while I knew I couldn't have done anything to prevent her cancer, there were always the accusing questions in my mind: *Did I do enough? Maybe I could have recognized some signs earlier? Was I not available enough to Pam? Did I do something to bring this on? Pam was always a hard worker—did I not help out around the house enough?* I searched for some reasons for this unexpected event in our life, but I could not come up with a good answer. We all do this in a cancer diagnosis. We question our involvement. Did I do something wrong? Was it my fault somehow? It has been my experience that, following a cancer diagnosis, people usually begin to ask questions about their responsibility in the cancer. I was no different. I questioned, too.

And now, I would have to tell Pam's mom and dad this news. Sorrow grips you when you hear bad news. I felt like I had been crying for a week straight, mostly by myself while driving down the road to meetings or appointments.

I rehearsed the conversation so many times on my way to the airport and each time I'd begin to weep uncontrollably. I yelled. I screamed. I prayed. I begged God for an immediate miracle. I thought about my kids and Pam's parents: "God, please don't let Pam die. Please!"

And then I arrived at the airport.

The flight arrived on time and I waited for Mom and Dad to come down the escalator. It seemed like an eternity before I spotted them, smiling faces as always. I smiled back at them, but behind my smile was a broken man.

"Hi Mom. Hi Dad." I gave them each a hug. "How was your trip?" I asked, trying to divert any questions they might have about our family. I didn't want to tell them Pam's news in the airport because I knew I wouldn't be able to hold back the tears.

So we chit chatted about their trip as we walked to the parking lot. I placed their suitcases in the back of the van and then opened up the sliding door to let them in the back seat. "I just need to talk with you both for a few moments before we get going," I began. I think Dad thought it was a little strange to have them sit in the back seat when the passenger seat was open. I squished in the seat with them and grabbed their hands. "Pam was diagnosed with cancer," I said. There was silence. Mom's face changed. That broad smile that looked so much like Pam's disappeared, and in its place, deep sadness. I can't remember all the words that were spoken. I just remember Mom hugging me and Dad joining in. The only words I do remember came from Dad. "Let's pray," he said. And we did—in the middle of our minivan.

I can't imagine the conversation between Pam's mom and dad following the news of their daughter's cancer diagnosis. The order doesn't make sense—for a daughter to get cancer before her parents. I don't know how many times I've heard people say, "I've lived long enough. I wish I could take the cancer for her." I certainly said that. I could not comprehend Pam having to go down this road. I'd witnessed its devastating effects in other people's lives. I didn't want that for her—for us.

Pam's parents had always been amazingly supportive of our family. They treated me like a son and invested in our children's lives with such intentionality. I expected nothing less now. And they stepped up to the plate in such practical ways. Before we knew it, they adjusted their schedule to spend time with us and especially helped out when Pam was recovering from chemotherapy. Her two sisters also found time away from their busy schedules and families to help out in our home. They were a godsend.

Pam's parents were always so gracious in asking how they could best help us without forcing themselves on us or offering opinions that were not helpful. We made decisions as a family, Pam and I and our kids. Her parents provided a supporting role that best suited us and together we worked at being a caring family during this difficult time. I knew this would impact all of us, not just our family, and it did. But engaging our extended family and inviting them to be present with us in a number of different ways was a very important anchor in our journey.

I know that not all people are as blessed as I was to have such amazing in-laws. Pam and I had come from similar cultural backgrounds, which made for a smooth transition into married life and family decisions. And where there were differences, I felt comfortable integrating some of Pam's unique cultural traditions into our family unit and vice versa. During a time of crisis is when the rubber hits the road in this synthesis of socialization and culture. Two family units that look at life differently, and yet understand and appreciate the uniqueness of the other, is crucial when life is turned upside down for one of its members.

Some families have a difficult time finding their unique identity because of very different cultural and family backgrounds. Everyone has heard the horror stories of meddling parents or relatives who try to control a family. Whether it is patriarchal or matriarchal structures, differing religions, expectations, roles or values, each component can cause discord. This is amplified when someone gets sick. Trouble can ensue quickly if boundaries are not established. Often it's not because people don't care. It's because certain families do things differently. The last thing that families need at a time of crisis is for conflict in cultural values to surface.

One of my goals as a counselor in working with couples who are getting married is to examine their cultural differences: the ways they were raised, their values, priorities, communication patterns, religious preferences, role expectations, etc. When you identify these differences, you can begin to take note of the areas that could surface and cause trouble and decide what to do with them when they do.

What I have discovered over and over again is that these differences often come to a boiling point during crisis. We revert to old patterns, and sometimes the things that are part of our family of origin can come back and cause problems in our current situation.

It's important to help families identify their internal differences and work with them, before those differences have dire consequences.

So it's important to accurately inform the extended family of the situation and let them know how they might be involved in the transition in a helpful and positive manner. Why do it at the outset? Because extended family, trying to be helpful, will sometimes rush in and make assumptions about what is needed. If you're clear about what you need — and don't need — you'll alleviate a lot of stress for everyone.

As you think about your extended family, think carefully about these important factors:

Communication patterns:
- Who is the primary communicator in your extended family?
- Do you want them to assume that role to help you out or not?
- Who will be the one who passes on information when you are exhausted?
- Who is that person in your extended family who often shows up in a crisis situation?
- What will their involvement with you look like now that cancer is a part of your life?

Spirituality:
- What about religion or spirituality?
- Is it important to your family?
- Is it important to you?
- Where do you want it to fit in to your new situation?
- There is often a leader in the family who steps into this role, so you need to decide who that might be?

Medical help:
- Do you have a family member who is experienced in the medical field?
- Will they be a source of good information for you, or would you rather focus on your present medical team?

Family of origin:

- Which members of the extended family want to stay and help?
- Is that who you want?
- What is the extended family's view surrounding cancer?
- Are they frightened of it?
- Have they had good experiences with doctors?
- What is the family history around cancer?
- Who might be calling you with unwanted "suggestions" that you may not want to speak with because of their past experience?
- Are there any pessimistic relatives you want to keep at a distance?
- Are there any positive relatives you want to include in your journey?

Have you spoken with your immediate family and asked for their input in the above? If not, it's a good idea to be on the same page as you consider this important anchor of extended family. Simply put, you'll need to consider who you want around you on your cancer journey. Who will inspire and encourage you and give you what you need internally and practically? Who will bring you down? You will want to think that through so you get what you need from family members.

In a later chapter on boundaries, you will be given some tools to help you be courageous enough to take a firm stand on what you need, but also sensitive enough to what others might need from you during the start of this journey. Anchors away!

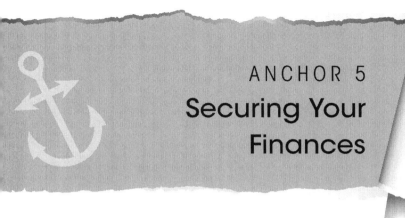

ANCHOR 5
Securing Your Finances

*The only thing money gives you is the
freedom of not worrying about money.*
– JOHNNY CARSON

I was already stretching our bank account as we continued to pay for our family home and build a cottage. In addition, raising four children who were heavy into competitive sports and music was pretty expensive. Who plans for an unexpected cancer diagnosis at a young age? Do you put aside a sum of money for this kind of event? I mean, I was planning ahead for a furnace, washing machine or water heater. But not cancer.

In my counseling practice, one of the first things I ask people following a diagnosis is about financial stability. We know that finances can be difficult in any family relationship, but what if it's compounded by a cancer diagnosis? It concerned me when I looked at my bank account and our family's needs. It was stressful. Perhaps you have gone through the same experience or you may be wondering right now how you're going to make ends meet.

Life does continue, even after an unexpected diagnosis. Groceries still need to be purchased, the mortgage requires the monthly payment, the car needs to have gas in it, and the children still need to have their physical needs met. Putting things in place at work is very important. Most people don't have the luxury of extended time away from work. How will you provide the extra care needed for someone with cancer who may be going through treatments or surgery?

Unfortunately, the work environment is not the easiest place to let people know what is happening in your life. "Keep your personal life separate from your work" seems to be a predominant mantra in many companies. If you are fortunate enough to have a few colleagues with whom you can share your circumstances, be grateful. It is a rarity.

Let's be honest here. How effective will you be at work in the midst of this new cancer story? You cannot be fully present no matter how hard you try. You will be constantly thinking of your loved one and that's normal.

We were doing well financially, but still had a growing family with many needs. As a marketing consultant, I worked away from home with some major clients. I owned my own business, and since I was self-employed, I had no company benefits as far as taking time off work. I *was* the company. Pam was a substitute teacher. So we had no benefits there either. I did not want to worry Pam about our finances, but I needed to be honest with my clients and what was going on in my life.

I decided from the very beginning not to hide Pam's cancer journey — which was *our* cancer journey as a family. I chose to be honest with all my clients about what was going on. They would, in turn, have to decide whether or not they wanted to work with me, based on my present circumstances.

I wanted to be available for Pam as much as possible. I knew our lives would change because of the treatments and subsequent recovery periods. I found honesty to the best policy. And I found empathy from strong businessmen who believed in me.

I have always been a person who tells people what is going on in my life, even if it's hard. I never did like to keep things in that could possibly impact my surroundings or other people. For me, cancer was not a private event. It was an experience to be shared openly with those who cared about me and about my life.

I do know people who have chosen to keep this a secret part of their lives. They feel that it may result in a negative outcome at work or used as a type of discrimination. They choose to keep silent about this event, not wanting to make it a big deal. Well… it IS a big deal!

When Pam was diagnosed with cancer, I was consulting for a company in Edmonton, a city one-hour south of where we lived. I knew immediately that Pam's surgery and pending chemotherapy treatments would change my work schedule. I needed to be close to her and to our children.

Kelly, the president of the company for which I was consulting, was renovating his building when I showed up to tell him the news of Pam's diagnosis. I had already thought ahead to some financial options prior to seeing him, believing that this specific contract would end this day. And I would certainly have understood if it had.

As I approached Kelly, I said to him somewhat tersely, "I have some difficult news." He looked at me. "Pam was diagnosed with cancer yesterday," I said. He stood there, speechless. "I will not be able to continue my contract with you since I need to be home with her. I'm so sorry." And then he surprised me. "You can work from home, Rick. Just come in once a week and let me know the progress on the project." I began to cry softly. The empathy of this man was so powerful that I was overwhelmed with emotion. "Are you sure?" I asked. "Yes, it's fine," he assured me. He was one of my major clients and to have lost that contract would have left us tight financially.

Three months later, I concluded my work with him, wondering how effective I had been at times. But he never said anything, he only supported me during this process. I will never forget the compassion of this man. Never.

I had to secure another job quickly following that con-tract—finances necessitated it. In my hometown, there was another businessman, known for his empathy, who gave me the flexibility to be with Pam whenever necessary. He gave us the gift of financial stability during Pam's times of treatment. The work environment is important and, since you spend many hours a day there, you need to decide how you will approach work, communicate with those who employ you, and be honest about your daily struggles.

Here are some things to consider, not only at work, but in light of new expenses that you may incur as a result of the cancer.

1   Speak openly with your boss about your situation.

2   Find out from your human resources department what ben-efits can be utilized.

3   Be honest regarding your availability and effectiveness at work if you are continuing to work (or if you are returning to work following treatment).

4   Decide how and when you will communicate the news with your co-workers.

5   Decide what you will say to your co-workers and how you will continue to share information along the way.

6   Readjust your financial decisions based upon your current situation.

7   Adjust your budget if necessary.

8   Find out which drugs you will need and how much will be covered under your benefit plan.

9   Ask others who have gone through cancer if they were surprised by any extra expenses.

Having financial security is a huge stress reliever for the one dealing with cancer and for the family unit. You don't need extra anxiety as you move into this journey. Plan now by making the necessary readjustments and let your family and friends in on what you will be doing to change things up for the time being.

Healing Your Past Relationships

*The weak can never forgive. Forgiveness
is the attribute of the strong.*

— MAHATMA GANDHI

When cancer comes crashing into our lives, it often unearths other life issues that compound the problem. It would be naive to say that a cancer diagnosis brings out the best in people. Unfortunately, it often highlights already existing problems that were there before the diagnosis. These challenges do not go away just because someone now has cancer. If you were struggling in your marriage before, it does not resolve itself because of cancer. If you were having difficulties with your teenage son, those difficulties will not go away after a cancer diagnosis. If you have not talked with a parent, friend, sibling or grandparent, a cancer diagnosis does not make everything right again. In fact, it can actually exacerbate the situation. If forgiveness doesn't come into play, you are whooped.

There is a powerful story from St. John's gospel account in the Bible. He describes a woman who has been caught in the act of adultery. A group of men are angrily clutching stones, ready to throw them at her — the legal punishment for her actions at that time. One of the men asks a question in an attempt to trick Jesus: "Teacher, this woman was caught in the act of adultery. The Law says to stone her. What do you say?"

The next thing Jesus does is brilliant. He stoops down and begins to write in the dust with his finger. What was he writing? We never find out from the text. Perhaps the secret sins of those who wanted to throw the stones? We don't know, but he knows that they are primed to make the punishment fit the crime so he says to them, "Go ahead, but let the one who has never sinned throw the first stone." And then he starts writing in the sand again. No one budged. Then slowly, one by one, from the oldest to the youngest (perhaps because the oldest knew they had more years of spiritual and moral infractions), they slowly walk away. Brilliant! Where does forgiveness start? With us being able to see our own brokenness.

When we are fighting a disease, we need every part of ourselves working on our side. Unresolved emotional turmoil as a result of strained relationships will impact our healing and living process. The more we have going for us from a heart, mind, soul and body perspective, the more advantages we will have as we enter and manage this cancer diagnosis.

Unforgiveness limits our ability to move forward. It's natural to throw the first stone at people who have hurt us. It's much harder to recognize our need to let go of the bitterness.

In one family situation I counseled, a patient's son said, "Don't let her into the room. Mom won't want to see her. She has not been involved in her life for years and now she comes back because of Mom's cancer?" I heard later that the patient and her sister had had a falling out years ago — angry words of disagreement that had never been resolved. So her children actually stood in the doorway and told their aunt to leave. I was shocked. Later I had a conversation with the lady in the hospital bed and she eventually invited her sister back. They patched things up as best they could—a past life of regrets.

Have you ever noticed how people come out of the woodwork when a tragedy—especially a life-threatening illness—hits? One big reason is guilt. Guilt because of something they have said or done that has left the relationship in a fragile state.

I have experienced this over and over again—the return of a family member or friend. You would think this might be the most inappropriate time to work things out from the past. But perhaps it's not.

There are many deep feelings that accompany a cancer diagnosis. I have seen people go one of two ways: they either harden their heart or they choose to soften their heart. The latter is obviously the better choice. The health benefits of "putting things right" is enormous. Research shows this over and over. Entering into a conversation in order to clear the air from past hurts lifts the stones from our hearts and the burdens that may have been there for a very long time. Sometimes it takes a defining moment like a terminal illness for us to take action around those things that we've been carrying.

So, how do you clear away the internal stones?

Are you ready for a formula that I have seen work many times, in all kinds of relationships and situations? Here it is:

You can clear the internal stones away by asking each person with whom you are currently out of relationship to forgive you first. *What? You've got to be kidding! I need to take the first steps, even when they have hurt me? Why?* Because it puts *you* in the driver's seat and allows you to take the steps that are best for *your* future health and happiness. We have all done things and contributed to misunderstandings. Asking for their forgiveness first lances the boil.

One counseling client came into my office and spent the first half hour complaining about his wife. She had been involved with another man twice during their marriage. That would be difficult. Rightly so, he was having trouble forgiving her. But he didn't want to leave her and he still loved her. I suggested he look at his own life first. I asked him to list the various ways in which he had possibly hurt, said or done things to his wife that were not helpful for the building of their marriage. In effect, I was asking him *not* to throw the first stone, as there are always two people involved in a relationship. His heart began to soften as he realized his own contribution to his wife's unhappiness. He went home and asked for her forgiveness. It was a turning point in their relationship. It softened his heart as well as hers.

If there is an opportunity to meet with people one-on-one to come clean, do it as quickly as you can. Some choose to use other methods to get to the place of forgiveness. These methods might be all that you have if the person who hurt you has died. Placing an empty chair in front of you and imagining the person to be there and then telling them what is going on inside you can be powerful, but has its obvious limitations. There is no substitute for the person-to-person interaction. Yes, it's scarier, but it's so much more freeing—softening hearts and allowing relationships to be renewed.

But what happens when someone chooses not to forgive you after you have been courageous enough to start the conversation?

You will likely have a few possible responses:

1. You might be angry.

When someone doesn't forgive you and you know they won't 'fess up to their own wrongdoing, there is a tendency to get really angry and feel betrayed. You took the initiative and now feel like the fool. But you aren't—you really aren't. You have shown great emotional intelligence in doing that. Be proud of yourself, even in the anger of having your vulnerability slighted. Walk away graciously.

2. You might be sad.

When someone doesn't forgive you and they have hurt you in numerous ways, you might feel sad. You were hoping this could have been a new beginning to the relationship — and it doesn't happen. You have made the effort and now you are just disappointed. Your hope of a new start has not materialized. Say, "Thank you for listening," and walk away. Then say to yourself, "I did something very significant in my life here. I can feel good about what just happened even if they didn't respond as expected — and maybe they will in the future."

3. You might express ambivalence… or worse!

If you feel hurt, perhaps your tendency is to throw your hands up and say something you might really regret. If you are tempted to lash out in words that are not helpful, instead say to the person, "I'm glad I was able to meet with you today. This was important for me to say. I won't be saying this again. I hope that someday you'll be able to accept this apology."

4. You might be embarrassed.

When the offended party refuses to forgive you, you may feel embarrassed by having taken the initiative. "Why did I do this? I just confessed. I came clean. Not only did she/he not admit their own guilt, they refused to forgive me. I have egg on my face now!" But what's so embarrassing about being the stronger of the two?

Prepare yourself to emotionally reframe what just happened. Don't go in with high expectations. Don't go into the conversation looking for a certain outcome. You took the high road. You took the first step. You may think they haven't heard you, but you've started something important. You never know what will come back to you from that conversation. You have the power to change the atmosphere by your response.

When you are lying on your deathbed years from now, you will be one of the courageous individuals who came clean and left life the way all of us should—with no stone unturned. You were one of the brave ones.

Go for it, you forgiveness warrior. Go into battle! You may have a few scars but you won't have any lasting or gaping wounds. And it's always easier to forgive others when you start with yourself first.

If you begin to see that you have not treated others as you would want to be treated, then forgiveness will come quickly to your life. Look at your own life first. Here's how to begin:

Practice Forgiveness

■ Take the first step. Don't be afraid to ask for their forgiveness first. Write down all the people that come to your mind who have hurt you in some way and who still may be part of your "clogged" heart.

Approach the person with whom you would like to clear the air. Consider using the following process as a guideline.
  • Words I said:
  • Acts I did:
  • Time I did not spend:
  • Support I should have given:
  • Experiences I am sorry for:

■ Ask for their forgiveness. Simply say, "I know I have not been perfect and have done some things that were unkind or thoughtless, and as I have shared them with you, I now ask for your forgiveness. Thank you for freeing me."

Then wait for their response back to you. If they do not respond, then you need to take action and let them know where they hurt you. Use the same process.
  • Words they said to you:
  • Acts they did to you:
  • Time they did not spend with you:
  • Support they should have given you:
  • Experiences they should regret with you:

- Now you can forgive them. Simply say, "I know you were not perfect and did some things that you would have done differently in hindsight. I just want you to know that you're off the hook. I forgive you."

Remember, not all people recognize the stones they have thrown at you. You can only approach them and hope they are open to recognizing the blockades they've contributed to your life.

You have taken the first step. You have been courageous and vulnerable. You are free to move out from underneath that burden and peacefully live life, knowing you have done all you can. A job well done!

ANCHOR 7
Finding Your Spiritual Pathway

If God is for us, who can be against us?
  – PAUL OF TARSUS

I used to take my children out fishing in our little paddleboat. We would find a spot on the lake, but the current would cause us to drift as we jigged for perch. The problem is that you can't jig well if you are moving. We decided to make an anchor out of an old paint can, filling it with cement and rocks. When we'd find a good fishing spot, we'd lower the paint can. It would secure us in one spot. That helped us catch the fish because we could see to the bottom of the shallow water and position our little hooks in the appropriate place.

You begin drifting when you are diagnosed with cancer — the unknowns are huge. You must use your anchors. If you don't, you'll feel out of control.

I believe that just below the surface of our circumstance, God is waiting for us to connect. For some people God is distant and for others, non-existent. For many, God is very much present.

I met a lady on a plane who told me she was going to a medium to help her connect with her loved one and with God. "Are you sure you need someone else to connect you to God?" I queried. "Maybe God is actually trying to connect with you and you just need to find out how you do that uniquely, in your own way." She seemed interested, so I continued. I asked if she had ever explored her spiritual pathway as suggested by author Gary Thomas in his book *Sacred Pathways*. I had found that book very helpful in exploring my own means of connecting to God. The concept of a spiritual pathway is a good start when considering who God is and who he wants to be in your life and your specific circumstance.

So often, people try to force their spiritual pathway upon another person. Have you ever had someone force their pathway to God on you and you just didn't understand their approach? "This is who God is and you need to understand God from this perspective!" ... and it made no sense to you. That's because you have your own way of experiencing God. And coming to a place where you are comfortable with who God is gives you a big anchor to stabilize you in your cancer journey.

There's an interesting story about Jesus of Nazareth — he's calling to some fishermen one day from the shores of the Sea of Galilee. He wants this swarthy group of fishermen to understand what he has to offer as a rabbi and teacher. They are having trouble catching fish that day, so he suggests they throw out their nets on the other side of the boat. They shrug, look at each other as if to say, "What have we got to lose?" and tried it. They're astonished! The catch is bigger than ever before. They figure there's something pretty unique about this guy, and Peter, one of the fishermen, says so. Jesus responds with, "Come and follow me and I will make you fishers of men." There it is — the invitation to discover something deeper about this man and his teachings. In the end, Peter takes him up on it.

Spirituality is the process of continually making us followers of something bigger than ourselves and connecting with something deeper than what presently exists in our life.

The knowledge that we were not abandoned to some mindless cosmic force was our family's biggest and most important anchor in the middle of the storm that was upon us. If you don't have this anchor, it's a good time to consider it in your life.

Would it be fair to say that when uncertainty occurs in our lives, it seems that we begin to search for answers? Often it includes what some have called a Higher Power, the Universe, or God. Whether people choose to use the word *religion* or *spirituality* has little bearing on the internal questions being asked. What is important is a person's openness to discovering something beyond himself or herself as he or she tries to make sense out of what is happening in their lives. As humans, we long for meaning — traumatic circumstances (in this case cancer) have us dialing a spiritual 911, as we search for a deeper understanding.

I have been with hundreds of people diagnosed with cancer and if they don't ask about the place of God in all of this stuff immediately, they eventually come to that question. I just wait and allow the deep thoughts to come forward in their own time and place. Here are some of the questions I hear most often:

- Where is God in this?
- Does God really care about what is happening to me?
- Can God heal?
- Are there such things as miracles?
- Why did this happen to me?
- What will happen to me if I die?
- Will God help me in my suffering?
- If God exists, why did this happen to me?
- Does prayer or meditation really work?

Even though some may have a strong faith prior to this challenge, many people still have a hard time understanding what has happened now that cancer is present and spreading. Their relationship with God can become strained. Some people even turn away from God. Most people who struggle with uncertainties, though, have the courage (and humility) to consider the place of God in their particular situation. For some who have not thought beyond the material world, they now decide to become proactive and get in touch with God out of desperation. I think God is fine with that.

People often ask me about my belief in God and I often invite them to discover it for themselves. While I do hold a certain understanding and experience of God, I would invite you to discover who God is uniquely for you at this particular juncture in your life, especially as you grapple with a cancer diagnosis. Often people who are struggling in life desire to understand the place and the importance of God in our lives, but wonder how to go deeper in experiencing God as real.

No two "faith journeys" are the same. God does the reaching and searching. Can you identify how God has been part of your life so far? And if you can't see God's involvement in your life, maybe this diagnosis will encourage you to take a closer look at God.

I have to admit, it forced me to look more deeply into God's place in my life. I was a Lutheran pastor turned businessman questioning where God was in Pam's cancer. It drove me deeper into conversation with the Divine and helped me to find peace, even though I couldn't understand and didn't have the answers.

I was brought up Lutheran, so I easily identified with a God who loved me unconditionally. I knew there was nothing I had done or that Pam had done to bring this on. It was not our 'sin' or lack of following God that gave Pam cancer. I knew God was for me and not against me. I figured he understood suffering better than I ever would, having given his son to die on my behalf. I knew that my relationship with God was based on faith and that somehow I needed to believe God was in the midst of all this stuff...but I still doubted. I stilled yelled at God. I still begged him to show up quickly and perform one of those miracles I had read about. This diagnosis and uncertainty drove me to a God who was waiting for me to see him more clearly.

Your spiritual journey is at a pivotal point. You can focus on God or you can throw spirituality to the wind. Perhaps this diagnosis might take you on a new adventure with God that you have not experienced before. For some it might even bring you back to God. It's an important consideration to make, even from the very onset of your journey.

I am not intending to buttonhole you into a particular pathway to connect with God, but I am challenging you to think about yours and be sensitive to others around you. "But I'm an atheist," you say. There is an old adage about war that says, "There are no atheists in foxholes." And if you have been diagnosed with cancer, you are indeed at war.

Your way may not be your friend's or family member's way. And that's okay.

Pam and I were different in our spiritual pathways. And so it was important that each of us honor the other's pathway as we began this journey together as husband and wife. We knew that God was significant in our lives, in our family structure and in our understanding of hope.

Pam was musical and sang beautifully. I met her in the choir as you'll recall, but she also sang in a small group back in college. I loved listening to her sing, because you could see how it connected her to Jesus. It was so evident, and when she sang about God, it's as if the spirit was touching our hearts, too. Often, when I would come home, music would be playing and Pam would be singing as she worked. She felt closest to God when there was music — as a result, she never wanted to miss a Sunday church service, even during her treatments or recovery. She was always there — three rows from the left, singing her heart out — her way of connecting with God.

I find God in the world and through my experiences with people. I sit in coffee shops, bars and hockey rinks and find myself talking about God with strangers who approach me. I learn about who God is for me through people stories, both good and difficult. I'm amazed at God's showing up in people's lives even when they don't know or expect it to happen. I know God is real. I see God working every day when I talk to people in my community.

Sitting alone in a quiet monastery, trying to find God through nature, or bringing about social change are not my spiritual pathways. It's crucial to recognize how each person meets God. It needs to be honored, especially as you go through this transition asking, "Is God really in this?"

Will you have the courage to explore spirituality in your life? Will you be vulnerable enough to ask questions and move out into an area of life that might not be that familiar to you? It's not about church — it's about Deep speaking to deep. It's about soul work. And each of us has a soul. And in our dark night of the soul, it's normal to ask questions.

So where do you start? Consider the following:

1. Intellectual thoughts about God

- This is who I think you are right now…
- This is what I don't understand about you…
- This is my experience so far with you…
- This is what I hear from others about you…

2. Personal thoughts about God

- This is what I am afraid of today…
- This is one big question I have right now…
- This is my major concern for a family member…
- This is the hardest thing to believe about you right now…

3. Faith thoughts about God

- I want to trust you with…
- I want to believe that you…

- I want to talk with (a person) about you...
- I want to hand over this part of my life to you right now...

Begin a daily discipline to put this anchor down in your life journey by being intentional and taking some actions that help you see beyond your human skills and initiatives to a God who is not just watching, but wants to sit beside you in this valley of your life.

Developing Your Attitude of Gratitude

Be careful what you think because your thoughts control your life.

– KING SOLOMON

E ach time our grandchildren come to visit us I learn something that only a child can teach me about priorities in living. For example, M&M's® have become synonymous with gratitude in my thinking because of my grandson, Connor, who loves trail mix. Well, not all the trail mix. He picks though the cashews, peanuts and raisins to find that which he deems sweetest — the M&M's®. "Look, Pa!" he says triumphantly, holding up the treasured chocolate candy that he discovered in the trail mix.

Pam was diagnosed with third stage cancer. That's a scary prognosis. How we talked to each other about it in the immediate family became very important. The words that we speak into our lives can either build up or bring down. This is not to say that we pull ourselves up by our bootstraps. No, we acknowledge realistically what is happening and choose to make every day, every moment count. Live bigger, not smaller.

Pam's enthusiastic and positive attitude was at the forefront of our family's mantra. She had this innate ability—she rarely complained about her life's circumstance nor did she criticize other people. In fact, gossip was strictly forbidden in our home and she enforced that. Was it repressive? No. It meant that negativity wasn't an option. People knew this about her—she wore it like a mantle and was well-loved in our community and neighborhood as a result.

We did decide it would be important to let the school administration and the children's teachers know of Pam's diagnosis and prognosis. That way, if the children seemed 'off' on a given day, their teachers would better understand what the kids were going through. We made appointments to meet with all of the teachers, coaches and leaders with whom they were involved.

Devon was in his final year of school and only a few weeks away from final exams when this news came about his mom. We went in to speak with the principal. He was sorry to hear our news and quickly suggested that Devon hold off on the exams, taking them in the summer when he was ready. "This would be a legitimate excuse," he assured us. Later that evening, we spoke with Devon and told him what the principal had said. Devon's quick response was to go ahead and take his exams because they would be crucial to his scholarship. Though he had the right to wait, he chose to take them and did well.

When I think back, I have often wondered why he would choose this option. And then I thought about his mom's attitude towards adversity—she lived the same way: head-on, without excuse, without hesitation, with a firm understanding that life continues even in the midst of unexpected brokenness.

All of the kids continued to engage in school, participate in sports, talk on the phone with their friends and have their little sibling fights along the way. All of us were watching the courage, tenacity and positive attitude of a mom on a journey with cancer.

It's pretty difficult to encourage a person to have a positive attitude following a difficult diagnosis. And yet the choice to find good in each day is an important principle. It impacts one's attitude toward their day and has a bearing on how others around them will interact. It changes the atmosphere.

I want to be careful in using the principle of positive thinking as the only important principle or ingredient necessary for you to live your life well. The truth is there are some people who have very positive attitudes and don't survive cancer. You can't always *will* your way into complete health as some suggest. And yet, we must also not underestimate the place of positive optimism in a cancer journey.

Jack Canfield in his book *The Success Principles* says, "You only have control over three things in your life: the thoughts you think; the images you visualize; and the action you take (your behavior)."[1]

You can develop and deepen your attitude of gratitude by daily reflecting on a few important principles. Examine each one for its place in your daily life.

- Do you surround yourself with people who believe in and affirm you?
- Do you choose to find something good in your day no matter what?
- Are you certain that you don't allow "I can't" to be part of your language?
- Do you affirm your life every day with positive self-talk?

Affirm your life every day with "I am." I am loved. I am smart. I am strong. I am going to grow from this experience. I am awesome because I am wonderfully made and have gifts and abilities. Reminding yourself of who you are will help you transition well.

Self-confidence is a significant trait in maintaining an optimistic view of life in the midst of difficulties. As a believer, my first trust is in God. But second is in the gifts and abilities God has placed in my life. All of us have gifts that can be utilized in our journey and one is the free will to choose what thoughts we will place in our mind.

Pam inspired us by her attitude and by her strong faith and confidence in God — she knew who she was. You could not help but be inspired by her optimistic and hopeful attitude. She lived each day to the fullest and her optimistic attitude rubbed off on all those who came in contact with her.

One of Pam's favorite television programs was *The Ellen DeGeneres Show*. Before her diagnosis, she rarely had an opportunity to watch TV, but as she began her chemo treatments, she was forced to rest at times. Sometimes if one of our daughters was home, they would cuddle in the bed and watch Ellen together. One day, Pam had just had a chemo treatment and was sick in the bathroom. She came out of the bathroom just in time for Ellen's dance at the beginning of the show. As the music began to play, Pam called out to Larissa, "It's starting! Come on! Let's dance!" and they went around the bedroom, laughing and dancing together. Only a few moments earlier, Pam was in the bathroom, heaving from the side effects of the drug that was trying to kill her cancer. Talk about a positive attitude changing your perception on life and impacting those around you!

Despite your life and its challenges, you can make a choice to bring a positive attitude to your day. For sure, some days will be harder than others and many days will require encouragement from a friend. Whatever flavor your given day is producing, you'll want to take 100% responsibility for your life, your decisions and your attitude.

If you need a little work on getting back your attitude, why not try some very simple exercise like those found below.

Choosing an attitude of gratitude:

Ask yourself the following questions. You may even want to write down your answers or share them with a trusted friend. Speaking them out loud can help create new thought patterns. Look back on your day and be surprised at what happened because of your intentional choices:

- What good thing, big or small, happened in my day?
- What surprised me?
- What made me smile?
- What person did something good in my life today?
- What can I be thankful for today?

ANCHOR 9
Helping Your Medical Team Help You

I suppose it is tempting, if the only tool you have is a hammer, to treat everything as if it were a nail.

- ABRAHAM MASLOW

The details about Pam's cancer were confusing. There are so many types of cancers, as well as a myriad of treatment options and drug combinations. We learned not to ask doctors what the chances are of the cancer disappearing, because they won't give you an answer. Doctors are focused on curing the disease. So unless you are set up with a palliative care doctor for end-of-life care, you will always be searching for answers.

When you are living with a cancer patient, you are living at the end of a pendulum all the time. Which way will it swing? It's really all about living life in the unknown. Even remission has a definition that is not easily defined or understandable.

Have you ever gone to the doctor's office and left more confused? Maybe you became very frustrated because you felt you didn't get straight answers to your questions. Maybe you even became angry. It has happened to all of us at one time or another.

Pam's medical professionals made a treatment plan according to her type of cancer. We needed to trust. We needed to believe. It was not easy because doctors are human and are making educated guesses based on history and research. What other options did we really have? I am not one to dig for information online, searching for every possibility. I have known many people who have done research on the Internet and have become even more confused. There is so much information available and you wonder what is accurate and what information can really be trusted.

At times, I did want to question what we were being told. I wanted to ask if they were doing all they could for Pam. We were told they would try other alternatives in the future, but for now we needed to trust them. That exacerbated my sense of helplessness.

I think, deep down, I wanted to ask the doctor my real question, "Is Pam going to die?" Lynn, Pam's twin sister, came with us to the doctor appointments initially because she had nurse's training. She was a second set of ears that understood the medical language. It is always good to have another person with you in these circumstances, especially when you are emotionally distraught and still in shock. It's a very confusing time.

We had a very kind doctor, although he didn't always answer our questions in a straightforward manner. "Third stage cancer requires aggressive treatment," the doctor said. "After you complete your surgery and you feel strong enough, we will start the chemotherapy treatments. It will be once a week for twelve weeks." "Three months of treatments," I thought to myself. "This is going to be a long haul for Pam."

Pam wanted to know everything about the disease and the plan that lay ahead for her. She was meticulous in her note taking. She always did things well, to her very best.

As we arrived home that first day, she checked the family calendar that hung in the kitchen, filled with all of the events of our family's life. She added her scheduled chemo treatments in the boxes for the next 12 weeks. To my amazement, she did not cross out any of the other scheduled events, she just simply added to what was already there.

There was no way she would take anything away from her family or friends. She would still walk with Michelle every Monday night, unless she wasn't feeling well. "Let's do life in the midst of all that is happening," she would say. And so that night, she would go for a walk with Michelle.

I think it's really important to keep on top of things medically during your initial diagnosis. That way you can begin to figure out the strategies necessary to managing life as best you can with this huge interruption. Some people may need an advocate to make calls for them and ask questions of the doctors and technicians on their behalf. Pam spent hours on the phone with nurses, receptionists and doctors getting her questions answered. She was kind but persistent.

I have been the advocate for many people in my profession as a pastor. Because of a variety of experiences that I've had over the years, I too have made phone calls when necessary or attended meetings as a second set of ears for people.

Remember, you are a client and you are paying for a professional to help you. They owe you the time and the attention to listen to you. Sometimes courageous conversations need to take place to put your mind at ease. If something is bothering you, it's important that the doctor hears you. You know your own body and your family knows you well, too. A good relationship with your medical team must include robust conversations that involve deep questions and open feedback that help you move forward in the best manner possible.

No conversations should be one-sided. There will be times when you will want to get more information and gain more understanding of a particular issue. You'll also want to give feedback or challenge a point of view of a member of the medical profession. Many patients refuse to enter this territory because they feel incompetent with medical language and see it as a potential conflict. "If I appear confrontational, I may not get the care I need," they think to themselves. Authentic and vulnerable relationships require frank conversations. By not having the conversation, you will leave the situation frustrated and unhappy. Doctors are people first. They are no different than you. They have been trained in a specific task. They have become experts in their fields. So being fearful of their response and choosing not to be "graciously proactive" can be detrimental to your treatment, leaving you in the dark. So help them help you.

Most people have difficulty with feedback. But I have found there are ways to ask questions that are wise and eliminate some of the possible patient-doctor conflict. In some cases, a "bad bedside manner" can actually be exacerbated by the patient or family member's abrasive stance. Consider how you ask your questions, and how a doctor could respond to your approach before you even ask. After all, as the Proverb goes, "a soft answer turns away wrath."

How would you want to be spoken to, questioned or respected? Patients and family members need to learn to ask good questions and doctors need to learn to give honest answers. Both need to be tempered with grace. When families are on this journey, emotions run high. The only way to get the answers and advice you need from medical staff is to build rapport. That doesn't happen if a person takes an adversarial stance against doctors, nurses and social workers.

Putting yourself in someone else's shoes is the best medicine for building rapport. How do YOU respond to feedback? Or questions that you feel challenge your integrity? We fear feedback from others because of the deep emotions that can potentially be triggered in our hearts.

Think about some of these situations for a moment. Perhaps they are familiar to you. Thinking back, what feeling began to rise up in your heart when you heard these words?

- I would like to talk to you about your performance at work.
- We need to discuss how much time you're spending with the children.
- I need to speak to you about your sermon today.
- We need to sit down and talk about your work ethic at school.
- I have some questions about the decision you made.
- I am going to get a second opinion.
- Is this all you can do?
- Should you be checking with other people about your work?

If any of these made you sweat, even a bit, imagine how your doctor feels. He or she is entrusted with the life of you or your family member. That's a lot of pressure! If you are intentional, purposeful and respectful in your questions, you will get the responses you need. The old adage, "you catch more flies with honey than with vinegar," is also true for your medical staff.

Trust is the key here. You probably don't know your doctor and the doctor doesn't know you. At first you are just his client, another number on a file that he or she has to deal with. It takes time to develop this relationship and for each party to be honest with one another.

I must admit, at first we felt like we were not getting the answers we wanted to our questions and it was very frustrating. Pam's doctor seemed rushed every time we went in for an appointment and we did not feel she was terribly sensitive to the situation. That was our perception — right or wrong.

But Pam was brilliant and saw a way to get what she needed. After a couple of appointments, she decided to provide a list of questions to the doctor prior to her coming into the room to examine her and talk with us. She would give this list of questions to the nurse before the appointment. The nurse in turn forwarded them to the doctor. When the doctor came in to meet with Pam, she answered them in order. It worked incredibly well. And the doctor would always end the conversation by asking, "Do you have any other questions?" The doctor's time was respected and we got our answers without becoming confrontational.

So how do you develop trust between two parties when you don't have much time to get to know each other? Pam would begin her "courageous conversations" with an emotional focus first. Here are some examples:

- "I'm feeling confused. I don't want to, but I wonder if you could help me..."
- "I'm feeling frightened that my body is not responding. Is this a normal response or should we be trying something different?"
- "I'm feeling sad that I'm not improving. My kids are asking questions about my body's response to this medication. What should I tell them?"

When you start with an emotion, it doesn't have to come out as a misplaced response later on. It's on the table to begin with and directs the rest of the conversation from that point on.

So instead of letting unexpressed emotions leak into the conversation, speaking with your body language instead of words, indulging in an unpleasant exchange of words — say what you feel from the start. Vulnerability is way better than passive aggression.

You don't need to deny that you have feelings of fear or worry and that you need help understanding your situation from the medical team. Gain the information by starting with the feelings and you'll be surprised at how your future relationship can and will change.

Before you go see the doctor next time, jot down the questions you have. Decide that you want to have deeper and more robust conversations with the medical staff. Begin with a feeling, then ask your questions. Own the emotion. Don't blame or accuse. You will find this to be a very effective anchor to put down.

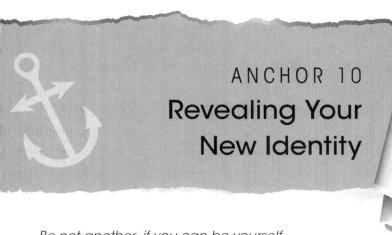

ANCHOR 10
Revealing Your New Identity

Be not another, if you can be yourself.
- PARACELSUS

The hysterectomy went well and the chemo visits were manageable. I went along with Pam for the first couple of treatments, but she also invited her friends to join her. The anti-nausea pills seemed to help and Pam was doing okay.

She came out of the bathroom one day with a clump of hair in her brush. It was time to shave off her hair. And she didn't hesitate.

I don't know how women can look so beautiful without hair, but Pam did. Maybe it was because of her vibrant smile, her composure, and her zest for life. But she managed to look stunning without hair.

She was a confident woman who realized her real worth was in her character and not her outer appearance.

It's almost as if she was teaching the world around her to look inside themselves to see real beauty. Somehow the external no longer mattered. Who she was on the inside was reflected in her outside. Our girls could never get Pam to buy new or expensive clothing.

She didn't need to. And even in her cancer journey, she was still a beautiful woman.

The cancer clinic had a list of people who would shave your head. They had given Pam the phone number for a place where she could both have her head shaved and choose a few wigs as well. "I don't need a wig," she said. "It's not me."

"I think I will call Anita," Pam said. Anita had always cut Pam's beautiful blond hair and she wanted to bring Anita into her journey. Pam was brilliant that way—she always used her situation as a teachable moment to everyone around her. She wasn't going to allow her cancer to impact the people in our small community in a negative way. She had cancer, not them.

She came home that evening with a bald head. Contrary to what you might think, we had a fun evening. The kids rubbed her head until it shone! And honestly, she looked great. I think it was because of her bright white smile. That's all you saw in Pam. Her smile that reached out to every person she met and made them feel loved.

"You know, Pam, you look really good!" I said. "You look like a female version of Mark Messier." For those of you non-hockey fans out there, Mark Messier was a famous Edmonton Oilers hockey player. "Of course, much more beautiful," I added. She just laughed.

Depending on her day and the temperature during the winter season, Pam would either wear one of the headscarves she had made, or go without entirely. The first day she went back to substitute teaching, she chose not to wear anything on her head. It was a teachable moment for every kid in that classroom as Pam was asked, "Mrs. Bergh, why don't you have any hair?"

Each person who battles cancer will find they have a new identity emerging. It's not that it changes who you are fundamentally. You are the same person, but there is a new and unexpected part of your life you never had before. Now you must choose to present it to the world in a way with which you are most comfortable.

There are many losses that can accompany a cancer diagnosis and each one impacts your identity in some unique way. If you are no longer working at a job outside the home, you have a new identity. If you were used to providing for your family financially and can no longer do that because you're struggling with cancer, then you have to get used to that shift as well. If you cannot make the sports games of your children now because of treatments, you have to shift the way you identify yourself as a parent who cares about your kids. If you have no hair on your head, you are revealing a part of yourself that is now missing. These all mean viewing yourself differently and working through the identity change.

Your roles may change and what has defined you in the past could look very different. Some people find it difficult to adapt to their new identity. Your self-perception is probably harder to deal with than the way others will see you.

Nevertheless, you now have the choice to present yourself in a new way to the world around you. This redefining of yourself will probably go beyond what you might have done in the past, and reflects even more accurately who you really are now. It's where the rubber meets the road.

Loss usually makes us stop and reflect: what do I want to be in the world now? It's not about performing for people and being something we aren't — it's about becoming even more authentic.

Pam was vulnerable in her cancer journey. She chose not to hide this part of herself. In fact, she would present it in a manner that would inspire people around her. She did this unwittingly — it was who she was. I suppose you could say she was comfortable in her own skin even though she was going through some pretty drastic physical changes.

Take time to examine some of the losses that may be occurring because of your cancer diagnosis. Consider the changes they will bring to your current life. What will you miss? And how will you adapt? Pam had to miss some of her children's activities, her weekly walks with a friend and an active sex life with her husband. Those are not easy switches to make when they are a big part of who you are.

Now it's your turn to examine what might be different for you and then I will help you step back and look at your identity differently. Who am I now? What am I missing? What will be new for me? What do I have to give up because of my cancer diagnosis?

1   Work   _____

2   Recreation _____

3   Family   _____

4   Finances   _____

5   Friendships _____

6   Physically _____

7   Leisure   _____

8   Spouse   _____

Acknowledge that these losses are important and are a result of something you had no control over.

Reframe quickly and say, "This is who I am now," and then decide what you will add to your life as a result of your diagnosis. For example, Pam read more books, watched more of her favorite television shows, cooked different recipes, and changed her bedtime to a lot earlier (she was a real night owl!). Some losses were bigger than others, but what she added was significant in her transition. There is enough being taken away from you when you have cancer, so add good things to your life that empower you and can change you in some beautiful ways.

What have you always wanted to do and now have the opportunity to do? Write them down. I will add this to my life …..

1

2

3

4

5

ANCHOR 11
Mobilizing Your Community

*It is only when we stand up, with all our failings
and sufferings, and try to support others
rather than withdraw into ourselves, that
we can fully live the life of community.*

– JEAN VANIER

We did not realize how many different casseroles existed in the cookbooks of the world! Living in a small community and belonging to a church equipped us with a freezer full of unending meals. We appreciated the meals, but I know the kids loved Friday night pizza more than ever after a week of casseroles.

Way beyond the great meals were the underlying unspoken words of support attached to the beef, chicken, fish, vegetable, pasta, and tofu casseroles that kept coming through our front door. What was spoken was really, "We love you." and "We care about you."

There is so much power in belonging. There is so much power in belonging in community. It starts when we are young, when we are searching for a place to find ourselves, outside of our own family. We look for a group of people who are similar to us, who value what is important to us and with whom we can become connected.

We need community. We were built for it. While our first community is our family, it's healthy to find other communities of people where we can expand our understanding of who we are. It's also a place to which we can contribute as well. We have an insatiable need to give of ourselves. That's all part of belonging. That's what it means to be hard-wired for relationship.

You only have to talk to people briefly and ask who they spend time with in order to discover what interest groups they most feel a part of and identify with. "They're like my second family," I have heard people say. This could be anything from service clubs, interest groups, an online community, church organizations, support groups, scrapbooking clubs, community choirs or sports teams.

These places become even more important to us following a cancer diagnosis. No one wants to be isolated—that's a living hell, even if you are an introvert. Meaningfulness and being known are two of the biggest ways to combat despair. And community offers that.

Have you ever experienced a time when a person in one of these communities was going through a hard time and you got together to support them in some way? They ended up in the hospital and you sent them flowers. There was a death in the family and you attended the funeral. They had an extended illness and you brought them dinner. They lost their job and you went for a visit. They discovered an illness and you asked if you could pray for them. You rallied around them because they were a part of the team, even though they may not be able to participate fully as they once did because of their situation.

I believe that finding a community has become even more important in our lives given our present-day individualistic society. Do you know your neighbor? Neighborhoods used to be very important and necessary for people. People used to know their neighbors, hang out together, share dinners, babysit kids, take each other to the hospital. Now more often than not, people are busy and tired, drive into their garage, close the door with their remote and stay inside their own world.

In Robert Putnam's book, *Bowling Alone*, he examines the decline of community in North American culture, compiling information from over 500,000 interviews that he conducted. His findings over the last 25 years show that North Americans meet with their families less frequently, are less involved in organizations, vote less, volunteer less, and don't know their next door neighbors. We even bowl alone. But we're built for relationship and meaningful experience.

Do you know your neighbors? Do you know anything more about them than when they take out the trash?

Many people do not know their neighbors and need an outside community to hang on to in difficult times. It's the *Cheers* model: a place where everybody knows your name…and then some. Most of this book was written at my little neighborhood pub called Cumbrian Arms. People know me there and ask about what I'm writing as I type frenetically on my iPad. They know my story and I know a few of theirs as well.

The cool thing about a community is that you can always choose how much you want to be involved in it and how much you want others to be involved in your life. You make that decision.

But why is community so important?

Staying involved in your community gives you a sense of normalcy in the midst of the shifting sands that you are experiencing. It gets you out of the house and out of your own head, just long enough to restore a sense of belonging.

A community can give you a perspective other than that of your family and close friends, who may be living too close to your situation. Within larger community, there could be others who have experienced a cancer diagnosis. Identifying with them could help you gain peace or a new understanding during a time when your world has been rocked.

Pam had a few strong communities that she belonged to. For her, the church was the most important community in her life and it reached out to us. Before we knew it, tons of prayers, prepared meals, and offers to drive Pam to appointments flooded into our home. To be surrounded by a living and gracious community is an amazing gift. She rarely missed going on Sundays, even during her treatments—she loved people and was loved in return.

Pam had also been involved in music, had sung in the community choir, lead Sparks, Brownies and Guides. Each community in its own way brought its care to the Bergh household. Pam continued to sing in the community choir, bald head and all. I loved it when she headed out the door to sing—she was so pumped and would come home elated from rehearsal.

I had my hockey team buddies and my close co-workers in addition to our church community. I was connected to a wider community, which was extremely helpful for me in our new situation.

How do you find a community if you don't have one?

- What are your interests or hobbies?
- What religious organizations would you consider being part of?
- What support groups are available in your community?
- Ask your friends about their extended communities?

Check out some and see if they would be a good fit for you. A community is more than one person, so perhaps just joining a small group of people would be helpful for you.

If you are entering into a new community, you need to be careful not to enter it with a taking attitude. You are not there to get something. You are there to be known, to contribute and to add value to the organization. In my many years as a pastor and counselor, I have experienced over and over again those who join an organization to take advantage of its members. You will not find the sense of belonging that you desire if you take that stance. We all know people who dominate the conversation with their problems. People will figure it our pretty quickly and you will feel even more lonely in the end.

If you don't feel that you are part of a strong community, don't let fear hold you back. Find one and belong to it as you are able. Yes, there will be times when you may not want to go to this community because of how you are feeling physically. And that's fair. But when you do, engage and be a part of it all.

I remember one lady who, following her cancer diagnosis, began to paint and joined an art club. It was a wonderful community that she became connected with and who supported her in some wonderful ways.

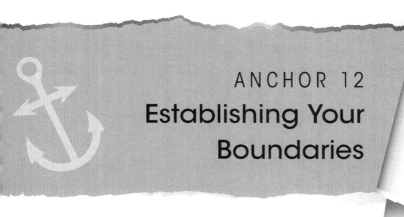

ANCHOR 12
Establishing Your Boundaries

Daring to set boundaries is about having the courage to love ourselves, even when we risk disappointing others.

– BRENÉ BROWN

"Stripe" was the stray cat who lived with us for 14 years while I was growing up. We loved her. So did the dog across the street. Or at least he usually did, until he came wandering into our yard one fateful day and discovered a very different cat than the one he had expected.

Like most homes in our neighborhood, we had a fenced yard with a gate at the front. The gate was usually closed, but for some reason, it was left open this particular day.

Stripe was pregnant. But this morning, she had something new to shows us. When we walked out into the backyard, she introduced us to five black and white kittens. None of them had the distinct stripe down the back that she had, but they sure were cute and had her coloring.

Normally, the dog across the street would tyrannize Stripe and we'd see her climb one of the many fruit trees to get away from the annoying hound. But today would be a little bit different. The dog decided to come for a visit, but his welcome was short-lived. As the dog came running toward Stripe (and her kittens), this overconfident dog got quite a surprise. Stripe bolted toward him, claws out and ready to pounce. He could smell trouble and quickly turned to run. But before he could get away, Stripe had jumped on his back and inched her way into his face with her claws. Once Stripe unhooked her claws and jumped off her attacker's back, the dog returned home, whipped and defeated, face bloodied, yelping all the way.

He never came back. Even when the gate was left wide open.

I tell this story to make a point about the importance of boundaries.

Something new and unexpected has happened. Cancer has entered the scene — unwanted and unplanned — but it's in your yard now.

Having boundaries is about having a sturdy fence around us. We need to know there is a gate that we can choose to open or close in order to let others into our experience.

Some will try to come in uninvited. Others will be invited and you will be happy to have them share in your experience. This is your choice. Creating boundaries around your experience is your work and responsibility, with the help of those close to you.

A boundary provides protection for you or your loved one who has been diagnosed with cancer and your family members who have received this news. Why do you need boundaries? Because we need protection. Just like the front door of our house, which we can choose to open or close, we need to be able to guard our hearts, time and resources, emotional and physical, when necessary.

At certain times we will need to help our loved one reinforce the boundaries they have agreed upon. The one fighting cancer is at times emotionally and physically exhausted. They have little energy to close the gate. We will need to help them at appropriate times. For example, I had to tell a few people not to come for a visit because Pam was exhausted from all of the attention. Having to tell people over and over again about her diagnosis was draining. Although she was gracious and always wanted to be accommodating, I soon became her gatekeeper.

By thinking back on the time when Pam was diagnosed and which boundaries I wish I had enforced as well as those I did put in place, I identified the following areas. You could probably add to the list and perhaps agree with some of these as well.

a) Curious Questions

It's hard when people are talking behind your back: "Did you hear? I heard that Robert has cancer? What's the prognosis? Is he holding up? I wonder how his kids are responding?" Creating a boundary means letting people know what is going on so there is no secondhand news. This minimizes gossip and puts rumors to rest.

b) Details

Needing to know the details of everything that's going on is a selfish request. We've all done it. Why do people need to know all the gritty details of our lives or treatment? Is that what's important? If we choose to share details, that's one thing, but we should never feel obligated to tell people. "I have cancer. I will be going through some treatments." Is that not enough? People don't need to know which treatment and when, nor what stage of cancer. The "less is more" principle is better when it comes to sharing details. Details that make you feel more in the know than others are counterfeits for genuine care.

c) Platitudes

Platitudes: things that people say that are supposed to make you feel better but actually make themselves feel better. Platitudes are really just a sign of insecurity and are an attempt to come up with appeasing answers. People must be so careful about these little 'nuggets of wisdom.' Often these involve people quoting religious sayings or scientific studies they've heard. They do this in an attempt to lighten the intensity of the moment, but they don't realize how infuriating it is to the one who's struggling.

d) Interference

When a person says that he or she can "totally relate" or "understands exactly" how the person diagnosed with cancer feels, they are interjecting their own story. Just because they have gone through something similar, doesn't mean they "get" how the cancer victim feels. My response to the statement, "I know exactly what you're going through," is to thank the person and remind them graciously that every situation is different—that if I have questions, I'll give them a call.

e) No

You need to learn when and how to say this word often and not be ashamed of it. You also need to have family members say it for you in order to fend off the people who want to drop over unexpectedly or phone for a conversation. Often their intent is not wrong—they just assume they are being helpful.

f) Medical

You have every right to ask questions and spend time with your doctor. You need to guide the conversation and ask whatever you feel is pertinent to your situation. You also have the right to make suggestions to your doctor and ask for his or her feedback. You may need to empower others to do this for you as you set up the parameters of this relationship.

g) Family

How close are you to your family? Some members may get involved quickly and try to be the heroes. Sometimes you may give in because you want the family to get along. This is a very tricky situation—a meddling knight in shining armor may not be the person you want around. You need to let them know their role and give them the reasons.

How are you with setting boundaries? Is it a difficult thing for you because you hate conflict—or are you ready to take on the world? Take this short quiz and consider how you may want to improve in this area of your life.

Boundaries Quiz

Try to be as honest as you can about the questions. Place yourself in the scenarios and choose your response quickly—don't think about it too much. Your first and natural response is usually the most accurate. Don't be embarrassed by your response to the questions. Recognize what they are and decide whether or not it is an area of your life you need to improve on. It's just being willing to gain skills that will help you now and in the future.

I   Your mother-in-law tells you that she's coming to help out tomorrow, but you need a few days to process the information about your wife's diagnosis.

    a)   I tell her she can come.
    b)   I ask her to wait for a few days.

2   Your doctor tells you that she will phone you when a date becomes
    available for surgery, but you want to try another option sooner.

    a)   I tell her that I will wait for her call.
    b)   I ask her what my other options might be.

3   Your boss tells you that a project is due on Monday, but it is the
    first scheduled chemo treatment for you wife.

    a)   I tell him that I will get it done and be there.
    b)   I let him know about the treatment and tell him I am able
         deliver after that.

4   While out for dinner, a friend tells you that traditional medicine
    is a waste of time and you need to consider going to Mexico.

    a)   I say nothing or say thank you.
    b)   I say, we are on a plan right now and I appreciate your support.

5   One of your friends apologizes that she has not phoned since the
    diagnosis and it's been weeks.

    a)   I say, "That's fine."
    b)   I say, "I'm disappointed because I really counted on you."

6   Your brother-in-law writes a nasty letter telling you that all of the family's life now revolves around your wife.

  a)   I ignore his letter.
  b)   I call a family meeting.

7   A religious friend tells you that God does not give you more than you can handle.

  a)   I keep silent or agree.
  b)   I say, "That has to do with temptation, not suffering and it isn't helpful."

8   A neighbor tells you they are coming over for a visit and you are tired.

  a)   I tell them to come on over.
  b)   I tell them it's not a good night and to come another time.

You have probably figured out by now that if you have good boundaries you would have answered B instead of A to each of these questions. How did you do? Do you need to be more proactive with your boundary setting? I can't emphasize enough what an important anchor this is to implement in your life, regardless of your situation.

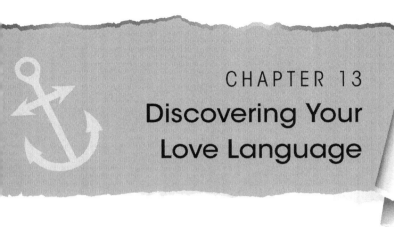

CHAPTER 13
Discovering Your Love Language

All of us blossom when we feel loved and wither when we do not feel loved.

— GARY CHAPMAN

had an old truck with two gas tanks. You would think that with two tanks there would always be one that would be filled, just in case the other one ran out of gas. But more often than I would like to admit, I ran both of them dry. Of course, I had a red gas can in the back of the truck, but sometimes that was empty as well. It's almost as if I had an attitude that with two, there would always be one filled and ready to go.

In our relationships, what if both of our love tanks are empty and we are trying hard to reach out and love each other? Gary Chapman's work on the *Five Love Languages* provides some of the most practical insights into filling an empty "love" tank.

Psychologists have concluded that the need to feel loved is our number one human need. What if we don't feel loved? What does that mean in terms of our relationships with people and our happiness? If we don't feel loved, how does that play out when we are going through big challenges in life? When difficult and traumatic circumstances interrupt life, the need to feel loved is crucial to our ongoing health, happiness and emotional stability.

Consider the power behind loving someone the way they understand it most. If a person asks for "oranges," they need oranges not "grapes," even if *you* think grapes are amazing. Those who have just experienced a cancer diagnosis need a lot of TLC, but the right kind. If their love language is physical touch, sending flowers when you could give them a hug seems illogical to them, even though you're trying to be thoughtful. We all need love, but there are different ways that we receive love and different ways we give love. Love is the gas that keeps us going in our lives and when our tank is low, it needs to be replenished.

I thought a lot about this as I considered the diagnosis of my wife and her need to feel loved by me, the most significant person in her life.

Dr. Gary Chapman theorizes that there are five unique ways people communicate and understand emotional love. These are based on our unique psychological makeup and the way our parents and other significant persons expressed love to us as children.[2]

Once understood and then communicated to each other, we are able to fill up the "love tank" of another that he says may be empty or require filling at different junctions of our lives. If we don't give that person their preferred way of feeling emotionally loved, then a person can actually feel empty inside.

The turmoil that accompanies a cancer diagnosis is deep and unraveling. The feelings of sadness, uncertainty, anger, loneliness, anxiety, loss of control, which may lead to forms of depression, need to be recognized and acknowledged as factors in our transition. We feel empty. We may feel like the ground is crumbling underneath us. We need some sense of stability. We need to feel secure in the midst of the big change that is in our life and our families' lives. Much of our security is conditional upon the emotional love that is extended to us from others.

Our emotional love tank can become empty very quickly. We need to know we are loved and accepted. The assurance that someone is committed to our wellbeing and that someone is cheering us on is crucial. But even more important than knowing this in our head is experiencing it from a person who is close to us. Everyone needs to have loving care expressed to them via their own love language. If they don't, they shrivel up on the inside.

I was introduced to Dr. Chapman's work when I was counseling people with marriage issues or who were preparing for marriage. The effectiveness of his research has led me to apply love languages to other areas of transition, include a cancer diagnosis. I have discovered that when people are at their lowest, they need to have love expressed to them in their own language. This insight has proven to be a very useful tool with amazing results.

It seems that often when we experience something difficult in our lives, and more specifically a cancer diagnosis, people from everywhere come out of the woodwork to extend compassion. The outpouring of love sometimes comes from unexpected places and people.

On the surface, this is a beautiful expression of care towards some-one who is hurting. However, without consideration for the person's love language, it may have very little impact. Truth be told, it can actually have the opposite effect and leave the one on the receiving end feeling empty despite all your efforts.

Don't lose heart here though — everyone expresses and receives love in a different way. It's just a matter of learning your own way of expressing love and then taking note of the other person's love language. It isn't rocket science and it can revolutionize the way you love others. If you are willing to learn another person's primary love language, you can become effective communicators of love and be part of the filling up process, helping a person with cancer transition onto more solid ground.

So what are these love languages? Dr. Chapman says there are five:

1. Words of Affirmation

For some people, verbal compliments or words of affirmation are powerful communicators of love. But our words have both the ability to build up or tear down, leaving that individual feeling either filled up or empty.

For the one with cancer, whose dominant love language is *Words of Affirmation*, what you say to them will mean everything. This person needs a cheerleader who can speak words of encouragement and hope into their lives. Here are some examples:

- "You are doing so well!"
- "I really love the way you are digging into life."
- "You are an amazing inspiration to me."
- "You are so strong and so positive."
- "I admire your tenacity."
- "I believe in you!"

When someone takes notice of what's important to us and affirms that part of our life, we feel emotionally connected to that other person, even if it's a brief comment or an affirming smile. You know the other person 'gets' you. So if you feel that way, why not find out what jazzes the person who has just had a cancer diagnosis — What are they proud of? What brings them joy and fulfillment? — and affirm that.

- "That was a fabulous meal you made!"
- "You're still working part time and doing really well."
- "Your home is spotless!"
- "You are really supportive of your kids' sports, aren't you?"

Words of Affirmation show that we believe in this person. We are giving them credit and praise—they are taking the bull by the horns. We are saying "Good job!" Even in the midst of a cancer diagnosis, kind words fill up a love tank and nurture emotional health.

2. Quality Time Spent

For other people, *Quality Time Spent* together is the key to filling up their love tank. This quality time must be focused and involve sympathetic conversation. If it is idle chat, then it won't serve its purpose.

Consider the stress, pressure, and emotions of the individual who has been diagnosed with cancer. While words of affirmation may focus on what we are *saying*, quality time focuses on what the other is *hearing*—it's all about understanding the thoughts, feelings and desires of the person with whom you are spending time. This is listening that is genuine and uninterrupted, focusing upon the heart of the individual.

When you shift your busy schedule to spend time with a person, he or she sees that you care about them, that you are interested in them and that you enjoy being together with them, even in this hard journey.

It does not necessarily matter what you are doing together—context is less important than content. It's that you are doing something with them and giving them your full and undivided attention.

Empathy is crucial for those with the *Quality Time Spent* love language. They need to hear: "I'm present. I am here. I'm not going anywhere. I care about what you are going through. I don't have my cell phone on. I won't be taken away from you during our focused time together."

3. Gifts

Some people value receiving gifts as a symbol that someone cares for them. Dr. Chapman underlines the importance of symbols as having emotional value. We aren't talking about expensive gifts here, but rather simple gifts that make a person feel special and valued. It's not the size nor the cost of the gift that is significant. It's the tangible item that can be held that says: "I am thinking about you. You are important to me."

Dr. Chapman says that most people's love language can be easily identified because it's the way they express love as well. In this case, a person whose love language is *gifts* will often be the giver of gifts. This person has been one of those who has given gifts to many people and will continue to do that in order to express their love in a meaningful way—according to what they value most. *Gifts* is perhaps one of the easiest love languages to work with because it's uncomplicated. It's never about the most expensive or the most luxurious gift. It's the thought that counts. It could be a simple card, one rose, a book, a letter, or a homemade craft. It does not matter.

For the one who has been diagnosed with cancer and whose primary love language is *Gifts*, it's easy to quickly and effectively fill up their love tank.

4. Acts of Service

Other people love to serve. This is the way they love others and receive love. They will be scurrying around the home, doing chores, cooking meals, offering to fix the neighbor's fence, cleaning the house and making a meal to bring to an elderly shut-in.

Reciprocally, when an act of service is offered to them, they feel loved by the other person. So a person diagnosed with cancer and whose love language is Acts of Service will truly appreciate what you do for them, the little things and the big things. They feel loved when you drive them to appointments, bring over a meal, shovel their sidewalk, or vacuum their house. They are thinking about what needs to be done, so if you fill in these roles for the time being, they feel very much loved.

One thing about Acts of Service types is they need to still be able to serve and not just be served. It's important not to take away everything from them, because serving is also their way of expressing love. When Pam was in the hospital recovering from her hysterectomy, she still had a need to help those around her. She folded blankets, made her own bed, helped clear dishes from her room — she liked serving and expressed her care that way to the nurses and other patients. It was natural for her so it never came across as cloying or independent, only as nurturing.

But Acts of Service people, who have just been diagnosed with cancer or another debilitating illness, will feel extremely cared for if you offer ways to help them manage their newfound challenges. As they come to terms with the diagnosis, contemplating pending surgery and recovery time, your involvement in serving is crucial. Here are some questions to ask:

- "What can I do to help you?"
- "Can you give me a list of the things that need to be done?"
- "What are some tasks that need to be completed today?"

We read of an incident when Jesus healed a woman who was sick — Peter's mother-in-law to be exact. As soon as Jesus healed her, she got up and made everybody dinner. It's obvious what her love language preference was. Servers feel best when they're serving. They also really appreciate it and feel loved when others serve them.

An *Acts of Service* love language has nothing to do with being bossy or demanding and everything to do with emotional connection and feeling loved. If a person asks for help with something, the help you give will fill their love tank. It's an emotional response for them.

5. Physical Touch

Have you ever noticed how some people prefer a hug instead of a compliment? They have a close social distance and put their hand on your shoulder when they talk to you? These are the people for whom Physical Touch most affects their sense of being valued.

Of course for a spouse, holding hands, kissing, embracing and sexual intimacy are all ways of communicating emotional love to one's partner. For individuals whose principle love language is Physical Touch, without it they feel unloved. With it their emotional tank is filled and they feel secure in the love of their spouse.

Other forms of touch are important and may not necessarily be expressed by a spouse but by another family member, friend or acquaintance. A warm hug, a handshake, a pat on the back, a cuddle of the couch — all signs of warmth to the person who most prefers physical touch.

Knowing a person's love language will give you more "bang for your buck" as you love on those who are hurting. The one diagnosed needs to be loved in a particular way, but so do the family members who are supporting and surrounding this person.

I've already mentioned that Pam's preferred love language was Acts of Service. I remember her staying up late at night to finish all of the home tasks: laundry, cleaning, kid's lunches, cookies for other, preparing for Brownies and her children's choir and early literacy program. She would work hard. She served us as a family and she served others as well.

I also know how much it meant to her when we helped out around the house, fulfilling our chore duties and systematically crossing things off that list on the fridge as we completed them. She liked to get things done, and if the kids and I didn't do something, she would. So I would get the car washed, the sidewalk shoveled and the vacuuming done before she got to it.

I had discovered early in our marriage that bringing roses home for our special anniversaries was not that important to Pam. Gift-giving was not the thing that turned her crank. She would say, "Thank you, Rick, but we could use that money on something else." Daisies were her favorite flower, probably because they were the most economical.

Pam was also a very confident individual and although I would praise her for her gifts and affirm her as a mother, she would just smile and give credit to God. She would remind me that I needed to be careful how much I affirmed the kids. "Too much is not good," she would say. "They might become conceited or develop a big ego."

Pam was always busy, and I would have to haul her away to get her to spend time alone. We didn't have a lot of money, so we would go on a date to a restaurant and order a big cinnamon bun and share it. It was usually a short date because she would be wondering about the kids and thinking about the things she needed to get done. Time Spent was not a big priority for her, but Acts of Service was. While Pam did like to cuddle (all of our family photos include us touching, holding hands or being close), Physical Touch would be her secondary love language next to Acts of Service.

It's interesting that even though Acts of Service was Pam's main love tank filler, it was difficult for her to give up a part of that control as people began to bring over meals, offer to clean the house, and fill in some of the natural acts of service during her initial treatments and recovering periods. But when she resigned herself, I felt that her emotional love tank was filled often and she was able to focus and to find the energy to recover between her treatments. In fact, she never missed a treatment because of low blood levels.

If you would like to discover your love language, Gary Chapman's book entitled The Five Love Languages is an excellent tool. In the back of the book you will find a quiz that will help you to discover the way that you best give and receive love. This will in turn help you to understand and express love in another person's preferred love language, effectively engaging them when they are feeling weak.

Knowing Your Personality's Impact

Thank you for making me so wonderfully complex.
Your workmanship is marvelous. How well I know it.
— KING DAVID

have always been a big fan of understanding, identifying and appreciating personality differences. They help us communicate and interact with people who are not like us. Who do you hang around with in your leisure time? Who do you have a difficult time with at work? What kinds of people sometimes irritate you? That answer is usually people that are different than we are. Those traits that make us unique also cause the most friction, angst and challenges. Nevertheless, understanding personality differences can help you manage, facilitate and stabilize relationships during stressful and uncertain times.

We all know there are many different kinds of people in this world. But are you interested in discovering why? A look at your unique personality is a good place to start.

I think it's important to see the cancer diagnosis from a team perspective. It impacts the one who has cancer, but the family is also affected and should be involved in the process. For us there was Pam who was carrying the load of cancer in her body, but there was also her husband Rick and her four children. We were together on this team and needed to understand how we could best work together.

Many people believe they know the person closest to them well and we should. But sometimes we may miss out on some of the finer details that might help us better interact with those who are closest to us.

Here are some questions to ask in light of the above comment.

- Would it be helpful to know whether the person diagnosed with cancer prefers to have people around them or to spend time alone, choosing a few close family or friends when necessary?
- Would it be helpful to know whether a person diagnosed with cancer is more likely to take information in about their situation in great detail or to look at the big picture possibilities?
- Would it be helpful to know a person diagnosed with cancer is more likely to immediately share their feelings about what is going on or needs to think through the process before talking or sharing with you at a later time?
- Would it be helpful to know that the person diagnosed with cancer is wanting to put things in order and complete tasks each day or is comfortable leaving some loose ends during their journey?

This is how Pam's personality preferences played out in her life during the days that followed her diagnosis.

Pam gets her energy from being alone. She needed her quiet space at different times. You would think that every person needs to be surrounded by others when going through uncertain and challenging times. Pam loved people, but she also enjoyed her own space. Too many people around would sap her energy—energy she needed as she prepared to go through treatments and recovery.

Pam's personality was such that she needed to know all the details of her illness and the various options available to her. She was all about the fine details. She had her appointments, pills, meals, and rides all planned out on the calendar for us to see. She requested and knew about every procedure, drug and side affect so she could plan out her next steps based on all the facts.

Pam could easily express her feelings but, with an introverted personality, preferred to share what she was going through with a few people whom she trusted and in an environment in which she was comfortable. This often took place with me late at night in our bedroom, or emailing her sister, or cuddling on the couch with her children, or on a private phone call with her parents or on a walk with a trusted friend.

Pam also had clear day-to-day tasks that needed to be accomplished. Things needing to be done and completed "today." She worked from a to-do list. She made decisions quickly and did not need to wait around for more information to get going in her life.

If you are at all familiar with the *Myers-Briggs Type Indicator®* *(MBTI)*, you will recognize that Pam is an ISFJ (Introvert Sensing Feeling Judging) in the 16 personality types. I have used MBTI® often in my counseling and find it an effective tool for understanding people and helping them understand themselves and others. As a certified MBTI® facilitator, I've used it in marriage preparation, grief work, conflict resolution, career assessment and consulting. If you would like more information about this useful tool, please go to www.rickbergh.com/personalitypreference/diagnosis/.

I am an extrovert—the person closest to Pam preferred to get his energy from being with people. And I was an extreme extrovert back then, who enjoyed being around people often. I wanted to be with

Pam as much as I could, but knew she also needed her space. At first I felt guilty leaving her alone, but she understood my needs as well. "Get going and be with your hockey friends tonight," she would say as she ushered me out the front door.

I don't need all the details before making a decision. I am very positive in my outlook on life and see the possibilities without needing the minutiae that can go with it. If Pam hadn't known this part of my personality, she could have mistaken it for not caring. But she knew details were not important to me. Details, on the other hand, were very important to Pam, so I needed to honor that in her life as she went through specifics over and over.

Because of my extroverted personality, I basically shared my feelings with anyone who would listen. It has always been easy for me to share my emotions. But I soon realized that sometimes I would have to be patient with Pam as she preferred a more intimate and quiet space in order to hear what was going on in my heart.

I was like Pam in that I'm a "git 'er done" kind of person. So we were both on board as far as finishing and completing tasks for the day. But because I am also a visionary, it meant that I had a new idea every day. Again, if you are familiar with the MBTI® tool, you will have already determined that I'm an ENFJ (Extroverted Intuitive Feeling Judging). So my personality in a nutshell is a visionary extrovert who feels deeply and likes to complete tasks. Details are not my thing.

So who you are? Here are some scenarios to consider in understanding your personality traits:

- Are you outgoing and the life of the party? Or do you prefer to stay home, reading or watching TV?
- Do you like being with a lot of people? Or just a few close friends?
- Are you generally calm? Or sometimes a little hyper, nervous or anxious?

- Do you like telling other people what to do? Or do you prefer following other people's instructions?
- Do you have a long-standing routine you like to follow? Or is every day a new experience and opportunity to try new ways of doing things?
- Are you curious about how things work? Or do you prefer to just use an item or tool and not worry about how it functions?
- Do you have a strong need to achieve (i.e. to make money, get the best job, be a professional or be the most popular in our group)? Or are you happy-go-lucky and laid-back?
- Do you tend to worry about doing your best on a given task? Or are you more relaxed, accepting that mistakes happen?

Each person's personality should be taken into consideration because it impacts the entire team or family. Knowing who you are and what you need can be a huge stabilizing factor in your cancer journey.

ANCHOR 15
Developing Your Emotional Intelligence

While we may not be able to control all that happens to us, we can control what happens inside us.

— BENJAMIN FRANKLIN

The admitting nurse said tersely, "You do know that you have third stage cancer?" I was caught off guard. We had simply asked for clarification on how many treatments people with a similar prognosis would normally go through. I was so pissed and Pam knew it. That's why she immediately grabbed my hand—as a sign to restrain my mouth from letting loose a barrage of expletives. Her eyebrows were raised as if to say, "Slow down, Rick!" Pam was a lot kinder than I—by a long shot!

Was it fair and appropriate for the nurse to say that to us as we entered into our early treatment regime? Not from my point of view. What hot feeling had me up in arms that day in the cancer clinic? Whatever it was, it was trying to take away my hope. We were not quitters by nature. We were not statistics. My wife was not a number. And for someone to even hint at her demise was not appropriate in my book.

Pam and I spoke about my angry feelings on the way home that day. We came to the conclusion that I was feeling angry because the nurse had a different view of life than me. We reminded ourselves where we put our future and hope. Not totally in medicine, nor statistics, nor doctors — but in God.

The next time we visited we interacted with that same nurse and she asked us how we were doing. This time, I was SO ready and responded, "We are doing great! We really trust that God is in all of this and we live day by day as all of us should!" (A little passive aggressive perhaps, but I wasn't going to be influenced by her fatalistic comment the week before!) The nurse just smiled — and Pam grabbed my hand in a tighter grip than the previous week, did the eyebrow thing again — and I knew I was done.

Some people seem to be able to manage their emotional responses to their situation and to other people very effectively. Others are not as successful. Why is that? Have you ever noticed how some people are able to process their feelings quickly and to move forward in their life more easily than others?

We learn emotional intelligence through observation of others. Our family of origin and significant adults in our life model it to us. So unless we have had good mentors or have taken the time to examine this in our own life through our many encounters, we may struggle with representing and understanding our emotions well.

People handle emotions so differently. Some keep their feelings close to them, rarely revealing what's going on inside, while others emotionally explode onto the nearest bystander. Neither method is effective or smart.

Emotionally intelligent people are able to take inventory of what they're feeling and examine how it's affecting them. They intentionally gather all the information, process it and then express it in a healthy and effective manner.

When cancer comes to visit a family, emotions become even more intense than in normal daily living. People are more sensitive because of the deep implications and uncertainty that cancer brings. It's emotionally draining to begin with, so any further interference from people can set us off quickly. I found this to be true of my own life once Pam was diagnosed. My emotional response to my surroundings — well, let's be honest here, mostly to people — was more edgy. I came to a place where I needed to take responsibility for those emotions, so they wouldn't pull me down or send me spinning into an unhealthy place that I would later regret.

Emotional Intelligence (EQ) is a key ingredient in maintaining stability in uncertain times. We need to learn how to manage our emotions, especially ones we consider 'hot' emotions. Have you ever walked away from a conversation and realized in retrospect what you could have said differently that would have been a far better response? Someone with a strong EQ is able to do that while the conversation is taking place. It requires a quick assessment of self and an ability to read the situation and the other person while in the middle of the discussion. Yes, some people are naturally more gifted at quickly summing up their own emotions, but it is a skill that can be learned nonetheless.

Emotions will come up — it's part of being human. Just as emergency lights on the dashboard of our car warn us of possible mechanical issues, emotions signal to us that something inside of us needs attention. Taking a sledgehammer to your car's dashboard to suppress the warning is not a good option for the long-run. The same is true of a hot emotion. The key is to learn to identify these feelings quickly (whether it's rage, guilt, anger, insecurity, etc.), not let them take over, and then respond to people or circumstances constructively. Contrary to popular belief, venting our emotions all over other people does not make us feel better — it just causes regrets and rifts in our relationships.

What can happen if emotions are not identified and dealt with?

- Unexpressed emotions leak into the conversation. The key is to manage them, not deny them.
- Unexpressed emotions make it difficult to listen to a conversation objectively. We become so absorbed in our own situation that it's hard to hear what others are really saying to us.
- Unexpressed emotions take a toll on your relationships because you are not fully present. You stop showing up as your authentic self.

What can you do that will help you understand other people's feelings and help you handle your own hot emotions when they come to the surface? You need a process that works for you consistently.

When a hot feeling rises up in you:

1   **Simmer and Settle:** Stand back and examine it before responding. Take time to simmer for a moment. Once you've stepped back and acknowledged its presence, start to ask what's behind the feeling?

2   **Admit and Ask:** Identify the feeling and name it. Say to yourself, "I feel angry. And it's not wrong to feel this emotion. There is a reason for it to exist. But I don't have to let it control my behavior." Then ask objectively, "What is this emotion really saying to me and why I am I so upset?"

3   **Discern and Decide**: Examine who it was that made the statement and why. Perhaps it was necessary for that person to get across a point that was important yet difficult. It may have been important or maybe not. You need to decide that, putting it within the context of the conversation. Don't

assume that it is about you or your situation or was intended as a putdown. Don't let your emotions get ahead of you. Peel them back gently. Be a good detective and discern objectively.

4   **Values and Virtues**: Know that sometimes the emotion you are feeling is hot because someone is challenging something that is important to you. One of your core values feels threatened and you feel like responding accordingly. You are likely not angry with the person, but with the fact they have disagreed with something you consider of value.

5   **Review and Reframe**: If you can review the context when the emotion happened, then you can also decide what to do with that emotion and reframe it. The fact that your "buttons were pushed," eliciting an emotional response, points to something important inside you. It can mean one of many things: Do you need to enforce a boundary? Do you need to change a behavior in yourself? Did someone once say the same thing to you with bad intentions?

Regardless what this hot emotion is telling you, you need to take control of it. No one can change another person, only themselves. But you can choose *your* emotions.

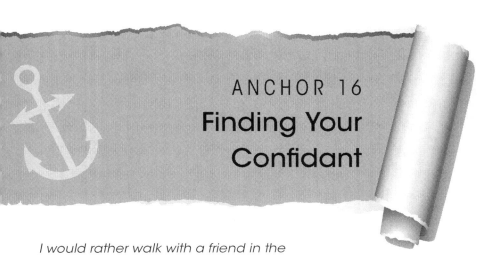

Finding Your Confidant

I would rather walk with a friend in the dark, than alone in the light.

– HELEN KELLER

One day my brother and I (ages 9 and 8) decided to take a shortcut home, which meant that we had to cross a field that was thick with mud from the spring rains. It would be the quickest route to the apartment where we were living. We were wearing rubber boots, but we did not realize was how deep, thick and bog-like the mud was on that field. About halfway home, I couldn't move another step — I was stuck — big time! The mud was like wet cement. My brother tried with all of his might to pull me out, but he couldn't. I was immovable. The mud was as high as the rim of my boots. I was in deep.

I had no choice but to leave the boots behind and walk home in my bare feet. I cried. But my brother held my hand and encouraged me to take one step at a time. It was cold out and I was soaked through, but I made it home eventually with his coaxing. My mom threw me in the bathtub — I had mud everywhere — my feet, my pants, my hands and all over my coat.

When my dad came home, my brother and I told him where the boots were. He went out and tried to find them. But it had continued to pour rain that day and when he went back to search for them, they had disappeared. Two boots lost in the mud. We never did find them.

It's easy to get stuck in our situation. And we can sink down even further if we don't surround ourselves with the right people. Choosing a friend with the right qualities is a smart decision.

Yes, I know what you are thinking. Even at the best of times, there are so many daily pressures that squeeze you dry — your energy and your time feel taxed to the max already. How much time do I really have left in my day to develop another close relationship outside my immediate family? All of this is true. After fulfilling commitments to our spouse, our children, our grandchildren, our job, we are often left feeling exhausted and overwhelmed.

So when you think about inviting a friend into your cancer journey, you may think it's just another thing to add to your already over-burdened life.

But what if you had a relationship that empowered you? A confidant who helped you sort out some of your unstable emotions? An extra ear to listen to your concerns? A person who could encourage and lighten you up when necessary? Someone to bring you perspective when making tough decisions? A friend who was truly open, honest and committed to you? Would you be interested in that kind of friend?

Don't just pick a friend who tells you all the wonderful things you want to hear about yourself. Your friend needs to be able to call you to task when necessary. Otherwise, you won't grow.

Consider the following questions as you evaluate whether you currently have this type of relationship in your life:

- Do you have a friend who encourages you in a specific area of your life?
- Can you think of a time when you shared a concern with a friend?
- Can you recall a time when a friend held you accountable to a goal that you set? Did they help you move forward in that goal?
- The last time you went through a crisis, did you have a good friend you could talk to about it?
- Do you have one good friend that you can count on no matter what?
- Do you have a friend to whom you could confess a wrong choice or an unhealthy behavior rather than keeping it secret?

Was your answer "yes" to most of these questions? Good for you! If not, would you be interested in discovering such a friend to walk with you during this time in your life?

Pam had Michelle, her best friend. They spent many hours together, sharing their hearts, fears, hopes and often tears. I don't know all the conversations that took place between these two best friends, but I suspect they were important.

Each week, as long as Pam was strong enough, they would venture out for their evening walks and share life together.

I also had a best friend. Lucien and I would spend important moments together building into each other's lives. I knew that I had a best friend who listened to my heart as I managed my family, finances, changes and emotions, especially in light of Pam's cancer diagnosis.

While family is really important relationally, they are too close to the situation to be objective. A friend will provide just enough separation to give you that different perspective when necessary.

The main quality to look for when finding a good friend to begin your cancer journey with is trust. Everything else flows out of trust. As you think about a friend you would like to join you on this journey, consider these trust-forming principles. What friend is trustworthy to you?

1. Do you have a friend who keeps his/her word?

Keeping your word is extremely important. Trust is developed as people learn they can count on you to deliver on your promises. Do you keep your word? What you say is important. However, how you act on your word is even more crucial. Your word has to be as valuable and unbreakable as a diamond. If you make a promise, keep it. Don't make promises you can't keep. Even if it is a small thing, canceling or failing to follow through on your word can create trust issues.

Think about the times when somebody has not come through on a promise or commitment. Phrases like: "He never showed up." "She was always late to meetings." "She didn't follow-through on her commitments." These speak volumes about trustworthiness.

As you enter into a new life with this cancer diagnosis, think about the friend you want to be part of your life. Has this friend followed through in the following areas? Simple ongoing actions build trust.

a)   Does this friend show up on time to meetings or appointments?

b)   Has this friend followed through on commitments they have made?

c)   Does this friend keep their word? Is he honest, letting people know if he is not available or can't attend a meeting or appointment? Does she always find an excuse?

d)   Does this friend, if late, apologize or just pass it off as not important?

You need a committed friend to be available for you or at the very least commit to a time to check in with you on a regular basis.

You need to be able to count on this person. If they let you down, it's a trust relationship quickly broken.

2. Do you have a friend that's brave enough to tell you the truth?

You must always tell the truth, graciously if need be. This is harder than it sounds. We want to believe we are telling the truth but surprisingly we find ourselves telling little white lies to protect something in our own life or a significant relationship that is close to us.

Sometimes people choose to change the facts — this is called *confabulation*. Do we conveniently leave out some information that does not support our position? Do we leave out important parts of the story behind the story?

Why shouldn't we lie, if we think it'll "protect" someone from the truth? If you tell a lie, even a small lie, or exaggerate a story, people will lose respect for you. How can they trust you if you lied to them? If people catch you in a lie they will not believe you in the future. They will not trust your word. By speaking the truth, you become much more trustworthy and people will come to see you as one who has integrity.

Choose a friend who is willing to tell you the truth and be willing to receive it back.

3. Do you have a friend who is transparent and with whom you can be transparent?

People will not trust you unless you learn to share yourself: the good, the bad and the ugly. You need to take a risk and be vulnerable if you want to develop a deep trust relationship.

Will you take the initiative to go first? Are you willing to take your mask off first? Are you willing to show your true self? This is who I am…. Are you being authentic? Owning your thoughts, beliefs, emotions and responses is a good start to being transparent. Avoid artificial roles or actions. If people realize that you aren't being yourself, they will distrust you. Appropriate vulnerability is a good trust gauge.

True Fact: Everyone has secrets. Instead of allowing this to cause friction in the relationship, set a simple boundary by saying, "I am not ready to share these feelings right now, but I promise they have nothing to do with you, so please honor my privacy for the time being." This is a good option. There will be a time for sharing at a deeper level as trust grows.

As you think about an authentic friendship, you will need to find a person who has an open heart and who is willing to share his or her concerns as well. Yes, you are the one who is hurting and struggling because of cancer. But remember, your friend has his/her struggles as well. You can also be a best friend back and, in fact, your cancer diagnosis and journey may provide some wisdom for your friend's circumstances that you were unaware of before. Remember that other people are transitioning through their own losses and your insights might become very useful for them.

4. Do you have a friend that will give without any strings attached?

While there will be mutual benefits for both individuals in the friendship, your attitude upon entering into this relationship will have a significant impact on the outcome. You need to be willing to give more than you receive. People need to know that you have their best interests at heart. You are not just looking out for yourself. Even in your cancer journey, it's not "all about you." Make sure that your motives are clean. People can tell if you are expecting something in return. Committing to give rather than take will translate into higher trust.

Sometimes the "strings attached" can come in the form of code-pendence, which is over-empathy. You need to be needed and you find a friend who is more needy than you. It helps you feel better about yourself and your situation. Beware of those types of expectations—they "look" empathic, but reap unhealthiness in the end.

5. Hold fast to confidentiality.

Nothing can tear apart a trusting relationship more quickly than breaking confidentiality. Your friendship needs to be protected and the conversations you share together must stay within the four walls.

Gossip or even revealing small bits of information outside of this confidential relationship can have dire consequences and possibly end a friendship.

Think twice before you share confidential information.

6. Walk the talk.

Show consistency in your own behavior. Your friend is looking at you. Are you honest, decent, respectable, loyal and fair with others? Integrity helps build trust.

Walk the talk. Maintain integrity between what you say and what you do. This will prove your authenticity.

Take a few moments to reflect upon the principle of trust as you think about what kind of friend you would like to invite to be part of this journey with you. Beside each principle below, write the name of a friend that fits this description.

a) Keep your word
b) Tell the truth
c) Be transparent
d) Give without any strings attached
e) Hold fast to confidentiality
f) Walk the talk

A friendship is important. Why don't you talk to a friend who has these qualities and ask them to commit more intentionally to walking with you in the days to follow. Tell them why you feel their friendship is important. And remind them that you also want to be available for them — that this is not a one-way relationship.

If you have a friend at the moment who is dragging you down, is negative, always has to one-up you or is arrogant — basically someone who brings out the worst in you — then you need to keep your distance or perhaps even consider cutting this relationship off for the time being. You know what friends you want in your life and what traits make you a bigger person and bring out the best in you.

It is also not a bad idea to limit your number of friends. You won't have the time or energy to build into all of them or have all of them as a part of your life as you start this cancer journey.

Find this special friend and talk to them soon, but don't spread yourself thin with too many.

ANCHOR 17
Planning Your Celebrations

Celebrate what you want to see more of.
– TOM PETERS

L augh a lot. If you don't learn to laugh and continue to celebrate day-to-day life, you will not take advantage of some very important healing in your cancer journey.

We celebrated with Pam when she came through her surgery. We celebrated with her as she went through the first treatment. I gave her a badge of courage. We let others know of her victories — big and small. Family members were always informed.

The concept of living in hope is crucial during transition and uncertainty. We can choose to inspire and build hope into our lives or not.

The only way to combat the blow that has been dealt — the cancer diagnosis — is to celebrate. Find reasons to celebrate life — not just the person who has the cancer, but life in general. Life continues and finding reasons to enjoy living are key to finding hope.

Family events, holidays and birthdays become even more special and festive. When you are stopped in your tracks by a cancer diagnosis, you gain a whole new perspective as to what's really important. The truth is, when cancer comes you don't always know the future, so you make the most of the present and value each day, each event.

Create rituals, symbols and rites of passage that will inspire hope. How do you do that? You laugh a lot — it's healing. You go overboard in celebrating significant events in each family member's life. This is actually a great way to live whether or not you have cancer hanging over your head.

Devon was going to be our first child to graduate from high school. Pam did it up well. We rented a small hall. We each wrote a speech to be delivered at the dinner. We had the banquet catered. We opened gifts. Pam was so excited to plan this event. I could hardly get her to rest following her cancer treatments. It was so special and it kept her going. It wasn't a cover-up for fear of the future either — it was just heartfelt celebrating by a mom who understood the value of living.

What's important is that you spend time together, get support in the midst of your journey and see life from the vantage point of relationships.

Whether you are the one with cancer or it's a family member, take note of how you can inspire hope through celebration.

As we settled in for a summer which would include Pam finishing her first round of treatments, we packed up our family and headed out to our cottage on the lake. "I should probably cancel our family reunion slated for August," I said to Pam. "No, we are not giving up on that!" she said defiantly. "That's too important for all our family." Each year we hosted a big family reunion, which was usually attended by 80+ relatives over a long weekend. I thought it would be a little difficult for Pam to manage, considering the intensity of the treatments, but she would have nothing to do with my suggestion. So we went ahead with it. It was a tradition we all looked forward to. It would also be the first time many of our uncles, aunts, cousins, nephews and nieces would have seen Pam since her diagnosis. I loved watching Pam with each one. And we enjoyed seeing our children live life to its fullest.

Even though Pam did not have her normal energy, she continued to be her usual positive and vibrant self who wouldn't allow this cancer to defeat her vigor for life or her ongoing love for her family and friends.

She still lathered suntan lotion on my brother's back, watered the flowers that bloomed in the pots on the deck and reminded me of the list that was adhered to the old fridge. "Yes, Pam, I will take care of that." "Thank you, honey," she replied, flashing her broad, white smile in my direction. I was still smitten and she knew it.

As people began to gather, one by one, for the reunion, Pam welcomed them with hugs. Our children bounced with enthusiasm to get the boat on the lake. As I watched all of this positive energy around me, it dawned on me: we had done some really good work in a short period of time. The anchors we put down had stabilized our life. Not only stabilized, but allowed us to move onward to experience all that was before us.

It had been three months from the initial diagnosis to the family reunion in August. Life had changed quickly for all of us, but we did some intentional work that would serve us well in the future. I think, deep down, each of us felt we had gone through the first round of a boxing match and had survived. We took a few hits, but we were not knocked out. We gained momentum because we had survived this beginning, and the anchors not only provided stability but also a confidence to move forward in our lives as a family and as individuals within that family unit.

We would need those anchors moving forward, because we were not quite finished with the cancer. It continued to fight for space in Pam's body.

We were as ready as we could be as we continued this journey. But what became so surprising to us was the amazing way all of us were being changed. We were learning to recognize the important things in life. We were learning by watching Pam live her life with this disease — a disease that originally grabbed her, but which she turned on and faced with an inner strength that was an inspiration to all of us.

Pam's experience brought a clarity to life I had not noticed before. For me, the cancer journey magnified what was really important and the things that mattered most. All these unexpected lessons started affecting my life and had such a huge impact that I was changed forever.

Notes

1   Jack Canfield, *The Success Principles* (New York, NY: Harper Collins Publishers, 2005), 8.

2   Gary Chapman, *The Five Love Languages* (Chicago, Illinois: Northfield Publishing, 1992, 1995, 2004), 16.

About the Author

The author of *Taking Notice* and *Looking Ahead*, Rick Bergh was born and raised in Alberta and educated at Augustana University College, University of Alberta, and Saskatoon Lutheran Theological Seminary.

He is a Certified Thanatologist (CT), a designation bestowed by the Association for Death Education and Counseling (ADEC) after rigorous study in the area of death, dying and grief. In addition to his counseling practice, Rick is an author and speaker and has been heard numerous times on national radio.

Rick's various career paths and colorful life experience have given him a unique vantage point in his work as a thanatologist, educator, counselor, speaker and author.

Rick's 30-year vocation as a parish pastor positioned him among people who were continually working out life as a result of normal and unexpected transitions. His practical approach to transition is a result of hundreds of hours spent with individuals who were working through their loss, both personal and family.

His work in the community over the years as a volunteer, sports coach, community counselor, educator and funeral officiant broadens his knowledge and experience as he engaged people in their everyday challenges, listening and learning from their powerful stories.

His career change from pastor to businessman afforded him the opportunity to travel the world, expanding his awareness of cultural differences and universal truths in the area of loss.

Rick has taken his astute people and business skills and applied them to his work with his clientele, providing practical and effective approaches to his transitional loss work.

His personal journey with his first wife, Pam, who was diagnosed with cancer at the age of 42, dying five years later, has shaped his principles and understanding of loss. He and his four children searched for healthy ways to move forward at a key time in their lives.

Connect with Rick and check out his many other resources at www.rickbergh.com.

Rick Bergh and his wife, Erica, live in Cochrane, Alberta, Canada, in the foothills of the Rocky Mountains.

CONTACT RICK

To get the latest *Finding Anchors* updates and resources, visit: www.rickbergh.com/findinganchors

Rick speaks frequently on the topics found in his insightful and practical book. He can deliver a keynote, half-day, or full-day version of its content, depending upon your needs. Please visit his speaking webpage at:

www.rickbergh.com/findinganchors/speaking

Cancer Diagnosis
30 Tips to Help You Land on Your Feet

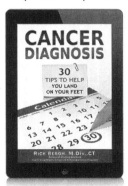

Please accept this free gift and then pass it on to those who are closest to you. I wrote this resource because, when we are diagnosed with cancer, most of us don't want to read reams of pages in search of information that will help us. We want practical insights that are concise and give practical help.

Go to www.rickbergh.com/cancertips for your free copy

All of Rick's resources are available at www.beaconmountpublishing.com

THE FINDING ANCHORS
DISCUSSION GUIDE SERIES

....reinforce the 17 ANCHORS with one or more from this series of interactive discussion guides.

Whether you are requiring...

- A resource to be used in your home with family
- A guide that will help form a community support group
- An educational tool to help your faith community become equipped
- Material to engage your clients in a counseling setting

...you will find a guide to meet your needs. For more details go to www.rickbergh.com/findinganchors/guides

All of Rick's resources are available at www.beaconmountpublishing.com

Taking Notice
How a Cancer Journey Can Magnify What's Important in Life

Transformational ideas are always in demand.

In this powerful book, Rick Bergh suggests that the most difficult challenges in your life are often your greatest teachers. We need to lean into them and learn from them.

Apply Rick's 17 "Lean Into Loss Principles" to any life transition and come out the other side with hope and a sense of new direction in your journey.

Looking Ahead
How Your Dying Impacts Those Around You

The ripple effect from your dying has a huge impact on those closest to you.

During his wife's final three months on earth, author, Rick Bergh, learned 17 very important lessons. In Looking Ahead he shares a framework for you to consider so that you and your family can make the most of your final days together.

All of Rick's resources are available at www.beaconmountpublishing.com

Made in the USA
Charleston, SC
11 October 2015